I0078703

STOP!

Or I'll Shoot!

This time it ends in homicide

Lakevia Amey

STOP! Or I'll Shoot!...This time it ends in homicide
Copyright © 2012 by Lakevia Amey

All rights reserved. No part of this book may be reproduced or transmitted in any form or by any means without written permission of the author.

ISBN-13: 978-0615674223
ISBN-10: 0615674224

Vienna Schilling Books
www.viennaschilling.us
Fair Oaks, California

Printed in the United States of America

Meet the Author

Lakevia Amey is a Los Angeles writer and ordained minister with life-experience in the topics she teaches about. Join Lakevia on her second, hot-button journey into truth, consequence and controversy. Her writing style is entertaining, probing and unapologetic.

This book is dedicated to the girl who lost her life at the hands of a church predator.

Preface

As the sequel to the first book I wrote, appropriately entitled *Predator*, this book continues to address the secret epidemic sexual immorality in the church. The first book was apparently a big hit because as soon as shipments came in, they were sold out. Perhaps this was because *Predator* did so with an in-your-face, unapologetic style that took the community by surprise.

Furthermore, *Predator* somehow fell into the hands of certain Catholic and Muslim women. They contacted me and said, "We never knew these remedies were available to us. We never saw them before!"

Hence, I saw the need for continued discussions on this subject. If you haven't already done so, you might want to pick up a copy of *Predator* and join in the discussion from the start. But I warn you; *Predator* was polite and constrained.

The gloves come off in this one.

LAKEVIA
AMEY

Why
fabulous
Christian
women can't
find love
in today's
church.

An
explosive
discussion
about sex
predators
prowling
Christian
singles.

4 STARS!
Honest, thought-provoking, troubling!
A great conversation for singles.
San Francisco Book Review

PREDATOR

Pick up a copy of Lakevia's first book today!
Visit www.lakevia.com

Table of Contents

Chapter 1

Modern-Day Paul

The Bible calls them wolves in sheep's clothing. I call them predators. Predators are people who use others to their advantage. They come in different shapes, sizes, colors, styles and forms, and can be either male or female. Predators prey on those who appear to be weak and their looks can be very deceiving. Their activities range from lying pathologically to rape and murder.

Many predators are draped in church robes, therefore, be on the lookout! They're everywhere; in schools, the work place and family picnics. They are even in churches standing right up there at the pulpit, so don't be surprised if you run into one any time soon.

Recently, the Lord showed me a vision. I saw a man; he was clean-cut and had on a white robe that reminded me of a choir robe. The clean-cut man looked like a pastor, but when I looked at his hands I saw long, sharp, blackened fingernails; as if he were some type of wolf.

It's easy to be deceived by a false prophet. The vision that I saw of this pastor seemed so real. He appeared to be anointed, and yet he deceived many. The only way I was able to tell that he was not right with God is because the Holy Spirit allowed me to see into the spiritual realm, otherwise I would have been blind like everyone else. Thanks to the Holy Spirit, I was able to detect a wolf.

Everyone is aware of the predator's existence, and yet they are allowed to continue to thrive. As you might know by now, my first book entitled *Predator* was released in late 2011, and is the prerequisite to this book. During my book-signings for *Predator*, several people asked me, "Don't you think that writing a book like *Predator* will run people out from the church?"

My answer was, "No, of course not. It will inform them and *stop them* from running out of the church. It arms them with information so they'll know what to do in case it happens to them!"

Because of *Predator,* they will be able to spot the situation immediately and either flee from it, or take action against it.

"Predator is nothing but a stern warning," I told them. Furthermore, if a minister tries to seduce an unsuspecting woman at his church, which is worse: the frank discussions in my books, or a pastor's hand up someone's dress?

I concluded that maybe it's a good idea for the victims in question to run out of churches like that, if it makes them feel safer on the outside!

It should also be noted that people who cover up the problem, allow the predator to thrive and attack other victims. In fact, their non-action disobeys the very instructions of the Lord. The proper way to deal with this epidemic is to confront it head on.

1st Timothy 5:20-21

Those who are sinning rebuke in the presence of all, so that all the rest may fear. I charge *you* before God and the Lord Jesus Christ and the elect angels that you observe these things without prejudice, doing nothing with partiality.

The contents of **Predator** are actually no different from the letters that the Apostle Paul wrote to the churches warning of this type of behavior. When the problem is confronted, we stop the denial.

The Apostle James said in Chapter 5:16 that the confession of sins is the first step to recovery. Even secular therapists know this, and still the church wants to cover things up?

The next step is to come up with a solution. The solution is to educate the saints and encourage them to feast on the word daily, so that when they are tempted by the enemy they will be able to defeat him with the word. Jesus said in Luke 4:4, "It is written: man does not live on bread alone." In other words, we can't live on physical food alone. Our spirits needs to be fed also. As believers we must feed our spirits with the word of God daily, so that we can mature as Christians. Throughout the entire passage, you will see that Jesus said repeatedly, "It is written...it is written...it is written." He defeated Satan with the word.

Many Christians get hurt by the church. As a result, they run away and many never return. It's not because they don't trust God; they just don't trust church people.

They have had bad experiences inside the church, so why would anyone in their right mind continue worshipping at a place where they have been hurt?

Back in 2011, my natural father shared a vision with me that the Lord showed him. My Dad said people were standing in a line, very happy and all dressed up, waiting to go into a particular church. As soon as they made it inside, they ran back out. My Dad said their hair stood straight up, as though they had been electrocuted. Something scared all those people out of their minds. Then, they took off running and never returned. Christ warned us that rogue elements would try to invade the Body of Christ.

Matthew 13:24-30

Jesus told them another parable: The kingdom of heaven is like a farmer (God) who sowed wheat (Christians) in his field (world). While he was sleeping, his enemy (Satan) came and sowed weeds (evil people) among the wheat. Soon the wheat sprouted and formed heads, but the weeds also appeared. The farmer's servants (angels) came to him and said, 'Sir, didn't you sow good seed in your field? Where did the weeds come from?"

And the owner replied, "An enemy has done this!" So the servants asked him, 'Sir, do you want us to go and destroy the field and start over?" But the farmer answered, "No, because while you are pulling up the weeds, you may uproot the wheat along with them. Let them both grow together until the harvest. First collect the weeds and tie them in bundles to be burned; then gather the wheat and bring it into my barn."

This parable serves as a warning to us all. During Old Testament times, Jewish citizens were easily recognized going into the temples and cities of Israel. During the New Testament age, however, converts come into the churches from all over the world and every walk of life. Because of the immense size of the Body of Christ on Earth today, it's much easier for counterfeits to slip in, who profess Christ in word, but not in truth. And this is present-day phenomena outlined in the parable above.

The good seed brought forth good fruit. True converts produce fruitful lives. False converts produce no fruit at all. Notice that the angels asked the Lord what should be done with these weeds, and the Lord warned that uprooting prematurely would damage the entire crop. And so the Lord allows the good and the evil to grow together, which means there will always be false professors among the true Christians until the time of judgment.

And so, in answer to those who do not agree that these two books should have ever been published, I will simply reply, "Just call me the modern day Paul."

What topics have I addressed that were not already covered by the Apostle Paul? I seem to recall one particular scathing event that plays out as one of the most scandalous things I've ever read!

1st Corinthians 5:1-5

Everyone has heard about the sexual immorality among you; something that not even Gentiles do! A man in your congregation is having sex with his father's wife? And, instead of expelling him from your community, you are actually proud of it. The next time you meet I will be with you in Spirit and the power of the Lord, at which time you are to expel that man from among you, for the destruction of his evil deeds, so that his soul might be saved.

Lakevia Amey

Any questions? Just call me the Modern Day Paul. Like Paul, I wrote these letters while on 'house arrest' to the attention of today's churches, concerning issues that need to be corrected.

The epidemic of church predators is causing too many people to run out of the church with their hair standing on end, and it's being swept under the rug by Christians! It's time to deal with these problems.

Some of you might take issue with the fact that I used a gun on the cover. Rest assured that the gun was used only as a metaphor, and is only meant to represent our spiritual weapons of warfare. If you recall, the Apostle Paul told us to put on daily the full armor of God, and the main weapon he mentioned was a rather deadly one; the spear. Like the gun, a spear doesn't care about distance. In a spit-second, the spear can impale a man at close range or thirty feet away. In street terms, both weapons can put a hole in you that they can't sew up! So, the gun merely represents a weapon of self-defense, to protect our lives, sanity, reputations and destiny.

My testimony is similar to that of Paul's. When I was on my way to persecute Christians, Christ appeared to me in a vision, just like he did with Paul. The man

8

started out as Saul and his name was then changed to Paul. I started out as La'Kevia, but my name has been changed to Evangelist Lakevia. Like Paul, I have been called to travel all around the world and go into the synagogues to preach the message that has been revealed to me.

At the appearance of Christ, Saul immediately surrendered to his authority and went into the city to await further orders. There, his blindness was healed, he received the Holy Spirit and accepted the believer's baptism. Likewise, before my conversion, I was spiritually blind, and now that I am in Christ, I can see. My eyes have been healed and are open to the things of God.

When Saul was in the world, he was a hot zealot for a religious god, and yet he was a seeker of the truth! Likewise, when I was out in the world, I never bought a lie; so why should I believe one now that I'm in Christ?

In the darkness I could not see anything. I was lost and could not find my way. Jesus is my flashlight which guides me out of darkness and into his marvelous light. Therefore, I owe him my life. Today, I'm a warrior employed by Christ, diligently seeking him.

I'm on a mission with the hope of winning
souls for Christ, and correcting those, with
love, who are in error.

Just call me the Modern-Day Paul.

Chapter 2

Green Card Predator

This time it ends in homicide.

My family attended a very small church in Long Beach, California, for years. The pastor there and his wife were very nice and we loved going there. One Sunday, my mother brought one of her friends to that church, and she, in turn, asked another friend to come along.

Before long, the second lady asked if she could bring her brother along also, and we said, "Sure, he can come too!"

Now, my mother was excited about bringing the lady's brother to church, thinking she was going to help bring a soul to Christ. He didn't have a church home, because he had just come from Africa.

Sunday finally arrived and the lady and her brother showed up for church. He seemed to be a gentle, well dressed and well mannered man.

He again came to church that next Sunday and the whole church family was excited to see him visit a second time. It seemed that he really enjoyed the services. When he showed up for Sunday service a third time, he wasted no time commencing his predatory game. He had set his radar upon a certain, attractive young woman who was a valued member of the church, and a good friend of mine.

However, our new guest didn't know who he was dealing with when it came to this particular friend of mine. Like me, she was not the type to be easily victimized and allow a predator to run his game. I cannot speculate as to why he targeted her because she did not have a weak disposition. If anything, she looked, acted, dressed and spoke as one who was 'in charge.'

Upon approaching my friend, he let her know, in no uncertain terms, that he was interested in her; but she told him right away that she was not interested in him.

Therefore, it was completely baffling as to why he decided to approach her again that following Sunday. Politely, she told him a second time that she was not interested.

On the way home from church, he informed my mother's friends about his ardent interest in my friend. I guess he thought my mother's friends would talk the woman into giving him a chance, but it didn't work.

We are now working on our fourth Sunday in question, whereupon my mother's friend approached the strong woman, and asked if she was aware of this man's interest in her, whereupon she informed them that she most certainly was, and had twice before turned him down. It seemed like he would not take no for an answer.

The woman then asked my mother's friend, "What do you know about him? He seems to be very aggressive; something's not right with him. It seems like his elevator does not go to the 5th floor."

Naturally, my mother's friend decided it was time to have a little talk with the young man. As she opened the subject with him, my strong friend and I watched from across the room. He became very angry with her. In fact, he became hot with anger, and his face looked as though it turned into a red-hot chili pepper!

Shortly after that, my mother's friend decided to go to the pastor to make him aware of the young man's behavior, so the pastor set aside time to have a long talk with him. That next Sunday he did show up for church again, but this time he got a ride from someone else. When he arrived at church he approached my strong friend again and began to speak to her in a very loud tone. In fact, he became quite aggressive.

As he aggressed against my friend, four deacons immediately surrounded him, including my father, and they were about to take that predator down. At that moment, my friend stood up to him one last time and told him, "No!"

Although he continued to go to church there, he finally realized that he had better leave my strong friend alone, and he acted as though nothing ever happened.

Shortly after that, my mother's friend decided to talk to the man's sister, and they spoke about his behavior. Instead of the man's sister seeing the gravity of the situation, she became extremely upset and stopped speaking to my mother's friend. Something in that family dynamic had obviously gone unaddressed.

It was now two months later, and we learned that he started preying on yet another young woman at our church. However, this next young lady also went to the pastor about him and the pastor spoke to him a second time. He finally realized that he wasn't going to accomplish his goal at this particular church so he left all together, empty-handed.

Our pastor handled the situation in an exemplary manner, and others in church leadership should take note.

Later we found out that he was trying to find someone to marry because his visa in the U.S. was about to expire. He would have to return to Africa, and he didn't want to go back. He preyed on the church because he knew Christian women want to get married, but he wasn't really looking for a wife; he was looking for a Green Card.

It was also obvious that his sister manipulated my mother and her friend, knowing they were Christians with an inside connection to women in the church. In the meantime, he found another local church to attend.

During this time, I worked as a stylist at a Los Angeles hair salon, and one day a pretty, young woman came in to get her hair done. She seemed very happy and kept a beautiful smile on her face; but when I started doing her hair she became very comfortable.

For some reason, women always seem to open up to their hairstylists; as though we become therapists. When she poured out her heart to me, I could not believe what I was hearing.

This pretty, young woman was not as happy as she appeared. At the time she was born, her mother was only twelve years old. At the age of just eleven, her young mother moved out and got a place with her boyfriend, leaving her alone in the house day in and day out.

When the young woman's godmother found out that the child was left at home alone, she took the little girl to come and live with her. However, the godmother's own son molested the child and started having sex with her on a regular basis, when she was just eleven!

As the young woman sat in my salon chair, she said that sex with this older boy was consensual, and that he did not force himself upon her. This was totally irrelevant to the situation and I told her so.

When her godmother discovered they were having sex, instead removing the little girl to safety, she took her to the doctor for birth control. At that point, I could not listen to anymore. I told the young woman, who by this point was already thirty-one years of age, that her god-mother was very out of line in the way she handled the situation. I said, "You were under age and I don't care how mature your body was. You were still a minor and it's easy to manipulate little girls. No eleven-year old is mature enough to engage in sexual intercourse."

I continued, "Your godmother should never have fit-ted you for birth control without your mothers' permis-sion." On the other hand, why should her young and reckless mother care if she was on birth control, or not?

From that point forward in the young woman's life, everything was a spiral downward. Every man she came in contact with basically used her for her body. She had been searching for love from the time she was born up to the age of thirty-one. All she ever wanted was to get married, have children and a family of her own.

She also expressed anxiety that her clock was ticking as though it were soon all over for her. And finally, she told me that she prayed and asked God to bless her with a husband and children. What happened next is mind-boggling.

My mother's friend and the African's sister were back on speaking terms, and that's how my mother learned of the news. The African man had gotten engaged to a young lady at his new church. We all wondered how he had gotten engaged so quickly since he left our church only two months earlier.

Short thereafter, the pretty, young woman came back into my salon, at which time she was genuinely excited about something. Bright-eyed she said, "You'll never guess what happened to me!"

She received a $50,000 court settlement of some sort...and she had gotten engaged!

Apparently, she met this gentleman at her church. They dated for just a few weeks, and he asked her to marry him. I was so very happy for her because this time she did not shed any tears while sitting in my chair!

I asked her to tell me his name and to my utter shock, her new fiancé was the African; the Green Card Predator.

He met her at his new church and saw that she was weak. Then he told her what she wanted to hear and she fell for it. I could not tell her what we experienced with this man at our own church, and that he was just using her for U.S. citizenship. She would never receive word of something like this coming from me. She would probably think I was jealous because I was still single, so on and so forth; therefore I said nothing.

Readers, we all know how women can get when they are in love. You cannot tell them anything.

My mother met the young lady at my hair salon one day, and we both felt very strongly that she needed to know what type of man she was dealing with, and again we never said anything.

Eventually, she was warned by someone else but, of course, she didn't receive the information that was presented to her. She believed the devil was trying to 'block her blessing.' This relationship was not of God. He does not 'bless' his daughters with predators.

One month later, her mother came into the salon and told us that the pretty, young woman was dead. She died at the age of just thirty-one. The L.A. County Coroner never determined the cause of death but her mother suspected foul play, and knowing the man's true character, so did we. When the coroner's office can't determine the cause of death, it's another way of saying...the murderer is really good at what he does.

I spoke to my mother's friend recently while writing the outline for this book, and she still remembers the African who came to our church looking for a wife. Apparently the man stalked her also after he left our church. She said, "He called me on the phone when all that was going on and told me everything that I did on this day and on that day. He called to let me know he was following me around and that I better watch out."

She continued, "The only thing he accomplished that day by calling me was scaring himself, because I reversed everything back on him and quoted scriptures until he hung up the phone. And I never heard from him again!"

I said, "He sounds like a real nut-case. You probably should have called the police."

She replied, "The only police I need is to call on Jesus!" I started laughing then, and of course she was right. Then, she quoted one of my favorite scriptures.

Isaiah 54:17

No weapon formed against me shall ever prosper, and any tongue that rises against me in judgment, I will condemn them!

Chapter 3

Open Prey

In 2006, I was very excited about becoming a member of a church that I had been visiting for about four months. One month after I became a member, a young lady joined the church who appeared to be on fire for the Lord, and she always stood up during testimony time every chance she got to give her testimony. It got to be so that we knew every last detail of her life!

This young lady spoke in tongues, was a single mother of three beautiful children, and appeared to be very anointed. However, she was living at a motel, her funds were running low, and she didn't have transportation. Still, it was always a pleasure to see her at church.

Everyone at church made sure that she at least received a ride home after church.

Now, this church had a shut-in prayer service one Friday night. The young woman attended and she again stood up to give her testimony. She had been married twice and her three children were a result of both marriages. What was so shocking to me is that both of her ex-husbands were clinically diagnosed as schizophrenics. She talked openly about "how hard it was being married to not one, but two nuts."

How in the world did she end up with two nuts?! After she finally escaped the first terrible marriage, she met her second husband. He wined and dined her, and provided for the children, but he forgot to mention that he was also a clinical schizophrenic. Hence, he knew all about what she went through with the first husband because of his own diagnosis, and yet he said nothing about it.

So she ended up marrying the second husband, and soon found out the hard way that he had the same problem. She and the kids ended up in a motel. When she left both husbands, the money supply ran out because the men in her life were her only source of income. Furthermore, the woman had also been sexually abused.

After listening to all of this, I thought to myself, she should be very careful because some of the men at this church might come along and take advantage of her all over again. She was just so vulnerable. She had a weak immune system and was in need of a healing.

Two Sundays later, she did not show up for church and I thought maybe she's sick, so I meant to ask her about this next time, but she never did come back to church. I was lead to pray for her because none of it seemed normal; that a young, vibrant woman so on fire for the Lord to suddenly stop coming to church for no apparent reason. Something was wrong and I could feel it in my spirit.

I continued to pray for her for months after that. One night, I had a dream that I was sitting in the front row at church, and I looked up on the pulpit. I saw a dark man sitting up there. I looked at him, and said, "The devil is on the pulpit."

Still in the vision, the man's eyes were now a glowing red. It seemed as though I were the only one who could see him. I woke up out of my sleep and was scared to go back to that church, but that next Sunday, I forced myself to go. All the ministers there were very friendly and would often greet members with a warm, brotherly hug at the door. Of course, there is nothing wrong with that. In fact, 1st Thessalonians 5:26 states, "Greet each other with a holy kiss."

A long time ago, instead of a kiss some cultures gave hugs and handshakes. In the Jewish synagogues of Paul's time, the kiss was a greeting of respect. The early Christians adopted this practice making it a holy kiss intended to show, not only love for one another, but for the Lord. In the early church, men greeted men and women greeted women. I think today's church should go back to doing things the way they were done in the early church to avoid problems.

Now, I did not feel comfortable hugging any of the ministers. Whenever they gave me a hug, I made sure to do so from the side and avoid frontal contact. Not every hug is a brotherly hug.

Men have been known to 'test' women by their hugs. If you don't want the hug to be too personal, make it quick and directed to the side of your body. And don't allow eye contact for too long. Shake hands firmly, greet them and keep it moving along.

During this time, I received a phone call one night from my natural father. Referring to the young mother of three living in the motel, he said, "Did you ever meet that new young lady who joined the church?" And I said, "Yes, I've been praying for her!"

He said, "Well, we found out why she hasn't been coming to church." He continued, "One of the married ministers has been having sex with her, so she stopped coming."

Sadly, the adultery was discovered by the adulterer's own wife. She reported the information to the pastor and he was dealt with. Okay, so wait for it...here it comes!

The minister in question actually came and stood before the entire congregation, confessed his sin, and then told the congregation that the Holy Spirit told him that the young woman living at the motel was supposed to be his true wife...not the one whom he was already married to!

It was an incident that gave new dimension to the word 'deceived.' The woman at the motel was ten years younger and thirty pounds lighter than his wife, and he just happened to be in the age-range wherein a lot of men go through male-menopause. His wife sat in the congregation that day as he stood making this so-called confession, but it was nothing but sin, and God hates sin.

What a way to represent for Christ! There was no light in that darkness at all. Imagine how his wife must have felt. The pastor sat him down for a season. He stopped coming to church, but his wife and children continued attending.

One day shortly after that, the minister in question walked into the church with the young lady from the motel on his arm, along with her children. It was as though they were a couple, and his first wife and children saw the whole thing! They were not yet divorced!

It was one of the most heartless acts I had ever seen and was purposely done. The Apostle Paul instructed us in 1st Corinthians 5:11-13 not to even EAT with someone like that. He should have been asked to leave immediately for showing such flagrant disrespect for his wife and children.

Be advised that God never gives one's spouse to another. That is considered adultery! If you believe that this incident was of the Lord, then you need to wake up and smell the coffee. Better yet, learn your scripture. Married men and women are off limits. It does not take a rocket scientist to figure that out.

Mark 10:9
What God has joined together [in marriage], let no man separate.

It turns out that the married minister in question was one of the 'nice guys' who gave her a ride back to the motel after services. Married men should never give single women rides anywhere, unless accompanied by his own wife. Deviating from the Lord's sound instructions on the rules of marriage only opens the door for chaos to come in.

We also found out later that he was the one who witnessed to her, and led her to come to the church in the first place. The predator minister in question ended up going back to his wife, and the pastor actually allowed him back on the pulpit. Shortly after that the pastor suspended him again. (Should we be surprised?) He often went out to witness to drug addicts and ended up getting addicted to drugs himself.

In the book **Predator** I discussed sharks feeding off blood. This young lady had never been healed. She was hemorrhaging uncontrollably all her life and that is why she continued to attract sharks. However, she foolishly allowed one shark to come in after another.

Notice also that she stood up often, practically at every meeting, to 'give her testimony.' It had become her way of 'begging.'

Like the woman with the issue of blood for twelve years, what she really needed to do was touch the garment of Jesus and stay in his ambulance until such time as she was fully recovered. The only way this type of curse can be broken is to place oneself in the able care of Jesus, and allow him to close up the hemorrhage so that sharks will no longer smell and attack.

Depending on how severe the offense is, it may take longer for the church to trust a perpetrator again. In extreme cases, some offenders should never be put back in leadership at all.

If a minister has been given time to prove himself and once again gains the trust of the church, that leader can be restored to a former position.

Ministers are like any other fallen believer. They can be restored to a former position. We must also remember that God does forgive. However, if that minister's recovery is not complete, it doesn't take long for the cracks to appear in his character's infrastructure.

1st Timothy 5:22
Do not lay hands on anyone suddenly, neither be partakers of another man's sins. Keep yourself pure.

The Apostle Paul cautioned young Timothy against being too quick to ordain a person. Doing so causes us to become partakers of this unqualified person's sin and to actually 'endorse' them if they act irresponsibly in office.

Ordination and appointments of position in the church mean to 'approve' of that one and his/her actions. Like Timothy, we must keep ourselves pure by not putting such persons into office, prematurely.

Chapter 4

Diabolique

In the summer of 2009, I ran into a man whom I met a decade earlier. We were both excited to see one another again after such a long time. I asked if he was a Christian, and he said, "Yes." In fact, he had become the senior pastor of his own church in Los Angeles.

We often talked on the phone and each time he happened to be on his way out the door to pray for someone, which gave me the impression that he was deeply immersed in ministry affairs. It was during these conversations that he confided in me that his father abandoned his mother when he was just a child, and it seemed like he could not forgive this event. Such trauma is usually the root cause of more serious dysfunctions.

I asked him why he was still single and he mentioned that he wanted to get married. I said, "Church is full of women and I'm surprised you have not met someone at church." He said, "I don't date women from church. It causes too many problems."

Okay, so that was a red flag. Whenever we hear a man say that he does not date women from his own church, *Run Forest Run,* because this means he is up to something. God has blessed many Christians with a mate from right there at their very own church, and we cannot put God in a box and limit his abilities. He can bless whomever, whenever, and however he pleases.

Usually, predators don't like to date women at their home church because they don't want the congregation to know what they are up to. It is also common for predators to date outside the church to cover up their activities. Or they might date one woman inside and another outside the church at the same time.

Now, whenever I talked with this old friend on the phone, I always spoke about the Lord, and noticed that he always changed the subject. One evening, he called me on the phone and I asked what he was doing at that moment. He said, "I just finished watching the football game, and now they're showing lingerie football."

'Lingerie football' is a new NFL half-time event wherein women come out on the field and play football basically in their drawers; hence the name 'lingerie football.'

So I asked, "Do they really come out on the field wearing nothing but lingerie?"

Quickly he replied, "Yes, and I wouldn't mind seeing you in lingerie!"

That's when I said, "As a man of God, you're out of order. You should watch what you say to women because you're in leadership now."

Then he became belligerent. He protested, "I know the word and I don't need you to preach to me!" Well, if he knew the word, why did he try to open an illicit conversation with me?

Another line predators like to use is the 'pride' defense. They'll say, "Remember that Psalm 16:18 says

'Pride goes before destruction, and a haughty spirit before a fall.'"

And that is exactly what he said at that moment. So I explained, "Hey, I'm correcting you out of brotherly love," whereupon he answered, "I feel like I can't be myself with you."

So I responded, "Well, you can be yourself, but if you are out of line, I will correct you," to which he responded, "You're way too serious! I can't even joke around with you. I could have said the same thing to a lot of women at the church and they would have laughed."

I said, "Something is wrong with that, and it sounds like the women at your church are probably carnal-minded, and so are you. What if God wants to elevate you by blessing you with a large ministry? Technically, those women could come forward and expose you. And that's why you need to watch what you say now."

Funny thing about words like...lingerie...massage... and...what are you wearing tonight. They always lead to other words like adultery...fornication...and lascivious acts. Such sins are craftily ushered in through subtle nuance at first, before long, things can get really filthy. Colossians 3:8 warns, "But now you must rid yourselves of all such things as these: anger, rage, malice, slander and filthy language from your lips."

Then I said, "What would you do if women at your church came forward and exposed you on your secret behavior?"

He got really quiet then and wanted to hang up. He tried to tempt me to see what he could get away with. God does not tempt us to sin. Matthew 6:13 states, "And lead us not into temptation but deliver us from the evil one."

The original Greek text states, "And lead us not into TESTING..." Hence, we know that God would never test or tempt us into sin.

Jesus instructed us to pray this, to show our complete dependence upon God for the power to overcome evil. Concerning my new phone-friend, I began wondering who his father really was; God or Satan? I recall talking with him about this in person, and he said something that might be both alarming and true.

"Christian women are the first to talk about what they will and will not do, but are the first ones to give it up!"

I thought to myself, *How would he know that? Have they given in to him many times already?*

I was proud of myself during this time, because I did not allow myself to be led into this trap. I learned that I had actually grown as a Christian. I forgave him for the 'lingerie' remark because that was the only time that he was out of line. He offered to take me out to lunch a couple of times, and I turned him down because I didn't know him that well, and I don't go places with just any-one, especially if they offer to drive. For all I know he could have been a reckless driver.

He said, "Why not? It's not like I will try something." I responded, "I know you won't because I 'm not going to give you a chance to."

About a month later, he invited me to his church's anniversary, where he was the senior pastor, and when I attended, I found that he actually preached a good mes-sage. I continued to visit the church every week, and I must admit, I really did enjoy the services. I also found the members to be nice, friendly people.

Before long my mother came with me, and she enjoyed the services so much, she had her clothes ready days in advance to attend. After four months of just visiting, we finally joined the church as members.

By this time, I considered him to be just the pastor, was not interested in him in a personal way, and I don't believe he was interested in me. We decided to become just friends. Eventually, twenty of our friends and family attended this church; therefore, what happened next impacted us all.

There was an attractive, young lady at the church who was always very friendly toward us. In fact, when she greeted my mother and me, she would say little things that caused us to believe she was the first lady...or something. In fact, after meeting her, I took a second look at the pastor's finger to make sure they weren't married.

One day after church I said, "Pastor, I thought you told me you were single." He said, "I am." I said, "Oh okay; well, it's no big deal. I'm only asking you because Sister So & So always greets us as though she's the first lady. Plus, she always sits in the second row directly behind you, and when we go on church outings both of you always show up in the same colors."

I saw them wearing matching colors many times, but I thought to myself, *He has no reason to lie. Maybe she's just one of those pastor-groupies.*

Even my mother noticed this and commented, "It seems as if Sister So & So is married to the pastor!"

I laughed out loud and my mother said, "What's so funny?" I said, "Mom, I was thinking the same thing!"

My mother said, "Well you know how women get when it comes to pastors, especially if they're single. Maybe she has a crush on him."

Soon thereafter, the church hosted a Mother's Day luncheon and I invited a young woman named Sparkle to the event. I introduced her to the pastor, and as she walked away he asked me, "Is Sparkle mean?" I responded, "No, maybe she's just tired or something."

Later that week, I ran into one of my guy-friends who gave me an inclination of things to come. He said, "Your new pastor is definitely called into ministry, but he's got some serious issues going on that he needs to deal with." He never told me what he meant by that.

Diabolique

Sparkle attended another Sunday morning service, whereupon the pastor greeted her with a big hug. I did not think anything of this because he always gives everyone hugs.

One Sunday night I prayed for the pastor right before I went to sleep. During my sleep, the Lord gave me a vision of the pastor stepping out of the church. In the vision, he walked down a few steps when his church robe fell off, exposing his worldly clothes.

Two different sets of clothing mean he is one way behind the pulpit, and another way when no one is looking. I never did let the pastor know what the Holy Spirit showed me.

Sparkle had not returned to church for a while after that, so the pastor came up to me and asked why. I said, "I don't know."

I found out later that he had been asking about Sparkle quite a lot. In fact, one of the other church members came up to me and asked, "Why does he keep asking about her?"

We both felt that he really should have been more careful. How does this look before the congregation?

Sparkle was not saved at this time; therefore, why should a pastor inquire about a woman whose spiritual condition was yet unknown to him?

A few months went by and Sparkle came into the salon to get her hair done. That day she told me, "Remember when I came to your church for Mother's Day? Well, shortly after that, your pastor contacted me on Facebook."

I asked, "Did you invite him to be your friend?"

And she said, "No, I thought you gave him my information."

I quickly assured her that I had done no such thing. He must have visited my Facebook page and noticed the link to Sparkle's page. Sparkle went on to say that she accepted his 'friend request' because he was my pastor.

She said, "I thought he wanted to invite me back to church!"

"Well, it's okay for a pastor to have Facebook friends, but if a pastor tries to hijack another member's friends without their permission, that's a serious problem."

Diabolique

I asked if he discussed church matters with her during their interaction on Facebook and she said, "No, he never did."

This means he contacted her with the wrong motives; not to mention the fact that Sparkle was not yet saved, which he also knew!

Then Sparkle said, "He asked me to meet him for lunch, and I just wanted to know what he wanted, so I went! When I got there, he said, 'The Holy Spirit told me that you're going to be my wife.'"

I was truly shocked.

Sparkle argued, "But I'm a heathen! Why would you want to marry me? I don't even go to church every Sunday!"

Ignoring her crisp logic he continued, "How do you feel about becoming a first lady?"

Sparkle replied, "I don't feel anything about it because I'm not going to become one. I don't like pastors and I would never marry a pastor!"

Then he told her that the Holy Spirit would put it into her spirit and teach her how to be a first lady. He had become diabolical.

Weeks before he preached against being unequally yoked in relationships, and how he could never marry someone that was not sold out for Christ.

Sparkle continued, "So, that's why I didn't come back to your church. I didn't want to tell you what happened because I know how faithful you are to Christ, and I didn't want to hurt you. After lunch that day, he contacted me several more times to get me to go out with him again. The last time I was at the church he gave me this really big hug and said, 'You don't know what you just did to me,'" she said with a disgusted face.

As Sparkle relayed the story, which seemed to get darker by the minute, I got sick to my stomach thinking about all the people in the congregation, as they jumped up and down, so elated by his 'sold out' sermons, and how they screamed and praised God at his preaching. The messages that he delivered, however, were totally contrary to his actions. Asking me why Sparkle hadn't come back to church was also a form of manipulation on his part. I continued to ask questions. "So, when he contacted you did he ask why you did not come back?"

She said, "No. That's why I don't go to church. A lot of those pastors are low down dirty dogs, and I'm not giving them my money. I can have church at home."

I said, "Not all pastors are like that, but pastors like him give all of them a bad name and cause people to run away from church."

I tried to salvage what was left of Sparkle's faith in God and said, "I want you to know one thing. God does not operate like that; only corrupt men do." But was there really any reason why she should have listened?

After Sparkle left the salon, I prayed for the pastor and asked God to lead me to another church home. I knew that my days were numbered there. I had to really force myself to go back to that church and the only reason I didn't leave right away was because I didn't want to slip into lethargy by sitting at home. The situation was just so disappointing.

A few weeks later, I started visiting another church, while the pastor continued emailing Sparkle on a regular basis. He was just that carnally-minded.

One foot in church and one out in the world; that's a rebellious spirit. 1st Samuel 15:23 states, "Rebellion is a form of witchcraft," and is totally out of the will of God.

His special brand of carnage continued right up to the time I left. On this particular day, he preached again about relationships from the pulpit. During this message, he told the congregation that he was not interested in marrying anyone from that congregation.

He said, "I don't want everyone up in my business!"

At that moment, the young lady in question (who greeted us as though she were his first lady) burst out crying uncontrollably in the middle of the service. The ushers ran over and handed her some tissues, where-upon she got up and ran out of church. She did not come back to that church for several months. And the pastor continued to contact Sparkle.

During one of those communications, Sparkle asked him why he kept contacting her when he's in a relation-ship with the young lady at the church. He denied it and then proceeded to make a slew of derogatory comments about her.

"No way, she's not my girlfriend! Look at how she dresses! She wears her skirts way too tight. Could you see me with someone that looks like that?"

Personally, I thought the young lady dressed very nicely. In fact, I often complimented her on how nice she looked and even asked where she purchased her outfits.

Then one day, his fall into darkness was witnessed by all. He had begun to preach compromising messages. Character flaws always come out in the wash. I can spot compromised messages a mile away.

During this particular one, he mentioned how tired he was of being single and that he's..."human, just like everyone else." Then, the man actually dared to say, "I have things on me that rise up too!"

I don't know where that came from because it had nothing to do with the Gospel. Not once did Jesus ever preach about having things that rise up on him, and how human he was. Therefore, is it acceptable to behave as such, just because one is not perfect?

Then, he began to preach how he would soon make a major decision and predicted that some of the members would probably get upset and leave. A few months later, the same young lady who ran out of the church crying, returned, and this time, she had an engagement ring on her finger. This carnally minded pastor had finally asked her to marry him.

In most cases, this is a time to celebrate and congratulate the happy couple, but my jaw dropped when I heard the news. I actually felt sorry for her. She had no idea about the many times he back-stabbed her about how unattractive she was, and how he could "never be seen with someone like that."

After the service, one of the sisters went over to congratulate the soon-to-be first lady and complimented her on how pretty she looked. "It looks like you lost weight," to which the pastor's fiancé replied, "I hope so, because pastor has been complaining about my skirts being too tight."

How would Sparkle know that information? Obviously, she had been telling the truth all along. When I got home, I spoke to Sparkle on the telephone.

"Maybe you won't hear from him anymore now that he's engaged to that girl."

Not so. The man called Sparkle minutes after I finished talking to her on the phone. Sparkle and I agreed he had a real sickness. He just wouldn't stop pursuing her, even after getting engaged!

In fact, he sent her a text and never mentioned anything about the engagement. Sparkle replied and sent him congratulations, to which he answered, "For what?" She texted back, "On your engagement."

He had the nerve to ask how she found out, followed by, "Thank you!"

This crazy man actually thought Sparkle would keep his devious activities a secret from my mother and me. He was so blinded by his own indiscretions, he didn't realize they were being advertized in front of all.

A few days later, Sparkle's family went on a vacation to Las Vegas. They called me from Vegas and said, "We need to talk to you when we come home."

The pastor had texted Sparkle with, "Help, Help, Help!" In other words, what did I get myself into by getting engaged? Sparkle let her mother see the message. The family was very upset by all this and felt sorry for the young woman whom he was engaged to.

He also texted Sparkle with, "I wish I was out there with you. We should have gone together."

Sparkle's mother refused to go back to that church. That weekend, the pastor announced to the congregation that he and 'the first lady' had run off and gotten married. To celebrate, the newlyweds invited the entire church out to lunch, but the pastor apparently snuck away for more texting. Sparkle received yet another text from him that was the most offensive of all.

"Let's run away together, baby."

She responded, "Run where?" He said, "Let's just run."

She replied, "Congratulations on the wedding."

He waited a few minutes and sent this one: "I still love you."

That was when I left the church for good. I attempted to talk to him about the whole situation three times before I left, which he avoided each time. He wanted to talk over the phone instead but I wanted to talk in person so that he could not hang up.

Chapter 5

Liar Liar,

Pants on Fire!

Anytime a man of God has to lie about being in a relationship with a woman at his church, something is very wrong. The reason I say this is because if you were to read about the fall of man in Genesis Chapter 3, the first thing Adam and Eve did after they ate from the Tree of Knowledge was lie about it. And then they tried to hide.

Notice also that they suddenly realized they were naked, and is the second reason they tried to hide. This shows us that the human brain comes with a guilt-chip, called the conscience, from which none of us can escape! In other words, when predators do wrong, they know it, but do it anyway. Whenever a man lies and hides about his activities, he is out of the will of God. He should repent and turn away from his sins. Christ will forgive him.

Women, if you are in a relationship with a man, Christian or not, who openly denies you, it's also a form of lying. Remember, if the Spirit of the Living God dwells in us, we should not tell lies. The reason is, Christ is not a liar. He is the truth and he cannot lie. And because his Spirit dwells in us, neither should we lie.

2nd Peter 2: 1-3

But there were also false prophets among the people, just as there will be false teachers among you. They will secretly introduce destructive heresies, even denying the sovereign Lord who purchased them, bringing quick destruction on themselves. Many will follow their shameful ways and will bring the way of truth into disrepute. In their greed these teachers will exploit you with stories they made up. Their condemnation has long been hanging over them, and their destruction has not been sleeping.

Liar Liar, Pants on Fire!

This particular passage tells us that one can always spot a false teacher because they camouflage their lies with half-truths, making it difficult to catch them. As discussed earlier, my natural father told me that the Lord showed him that the pastor, highlighted in the prior chapter, would try to hit on Sparkle. Because of predators like this, let's review Peter's warning in the verses:

1) Expect that there will be false teachers
2) Always be discerning with your eyes wide open
3) Watch for those who twist the truth about Christ; denying the sovereign Lord
4) Watch for those with shameful conduct
5) Watch for those with lust for money, power and exploitation

1st John 4:1

Dear friends, do not believe every spirit, but test the spirits to see whether they are from God, because many false prophets have gone out into the world.

Here, the Apostle John warns us that there are plenty of spirits (characters) who will try to destroy us. Besides evil, supernatural powers, deceptive humans walk among us as well, in whom the evil spirits operate. John wants believers to use their minds as well as their hearts.

> Far too many con-artists and counterfeiters are supported by unsuspecting Christians and knowing accomplices!

As discussed in the prior chapter, about twenty of my friends and family members were impacted by this pastor's conduct. He would often pray for God to add to the church and each month members were indeed added. However, many people left shortly thereafter because of his behavior. Each one of those members would have brought additional members but he thwarted his own church's growth with his conduct.

I am again reminded of the vision that God gave to my natural father. In the vision, my Dad saw many people in a line waiting to enter a church, all dressed up and happy to go inside, but once they finally got in, they ran out with their hair standing up on end, as though they had been electrocuted! They were scared out of their minds because of what they witnessed inside the church. I was one of those who ran out with my hair electrocuted.

I remember one Wednesday night the pastor in question taught on Jezebel. He spoke against everything that he was actually doing outside the church. He opened the forum for questions, so I raised my hand. I said, "What about married men who send emails to other women without their wives' knowledge? Is that considered a Jezebel spirit?"

Before he could answer, his new wife raised her hand and said "Yes!" Then he replied with a straight face, "Yes, the Jezebel spirit can work through a man or woman, and it's a spirit that runs rampant in the church!"

If you would like to read more on the sickening and destructive power of the Jezebel spirit, please read the Book of 1st Kings, Chapters 16 to 21. This particular demon can cause wholesale bloodshed and murder, and is not to be taken lightly.

Lakevia Amey

I learned to watch, pray, listen and wait. I am a watchman for Christ; one who has been chosen to watch out for sharks. Remember at the beginning of the last chapter, the pastor in question also tried to engage me in an inappropriate conversation that could have lead to filthy waters. Filthy waters represent sin. I would have been swimming in filthy water.

A servant of God should never be caught swimming in filthy, muddy water. Whenever we go swimming, the water should be clear, fresh and clean. Clear water represents the Holy Spirit. If the water is so dark that it looks like muddy, storm water, run for your life.

Remember also that he tried to get me to go to lunch with him and I declined because he was driving. As such, he might have been a reckless driver, since he was particularly reckless with his own life and calling.

A reckless driver is a one who steers without the Holy Spirit. He is not lead by the spirit; he is lead by the flesh. This is tantamount to drinking and driving. He is under the wrong influence while driving, which could lead to a fatal accident.

Liar Liar, Pants on Fire!

We have all heard about car accidents where everyone dies, except the driver. Innocent lives are destroyed all the time because one driver decides to drink alcohol and then get behind the wheel of a moving, two-ton vehicle (or worse).

I always ask myself, "Why did those people get into the car? They knew he was under the influence and their lives could have been spared!"

Watch whom you let drive your spirit. I learned how to swim on my own. Today, I have an excellent teacher, Christ Jesus. That's why I worship him. He's the one that keeps me afloat. With him I will never sink. With him, sharks might come close but, they will not attack.

Notice that when you go to the beach there is always a warning sign near the water that reads, "Danger Zone. Do not go past this point." The Holy Spirit warns his children the same way.

In Australia ten tourists die every summer in the wild surf surrounding that continent. Those people lost their lives for only one reason. They swam outside the flags, thinking they knew better than the Australian lifeguards, and toyed with their own lives. The violent surf outside the flags sucked them right out to sea, never to be seen or heard from again. In many cases, no one ever realized they were gone until hours later.

Now, I may be a good swimmer but, if I'm caught off guard, I could get bitten by a shark. "Get out of the water!" shouts the Holy Spirit. "The current is too strong!" Even a well trained swimmer could drown.

A loving master will always warn his servant because he wants to protect them from harm. His job is to provide everything that his servants need, including sound advice.

Listen to the voice of the Lord when he speaks! This is what gets the saints into trouble: when they heed their own emotions and not the voice of the Lord. The Holy Spirit speaks in many different ways. He can speak to our spirits, through his written word, through the word of a prophet, prayer, and signs and wonders. That is why it is so important for believers to have a daily prayer life. He can also give us visions and dreams along with the interpretation.

Apparently the pastor in the prior chapter was a shark who did not have any teeth because he walked away empty handed. He did not get the human meat that he wanted. Sparkle would not become his mistress and his marriage ended as well in less than a year. He was left with the word of God alone, which is the best meat any man can ever eat.

Eventually, he realized that he made some serious mistakes. He seemed to pride himself on being a shark, but while he was busy attacking, he was the one that got bitten in the process.

Eventually, he repented, was healed and delivered in the process. He was restored, and came back stronger than ever, and everyone moved on with their lives.

Chapter 6

Bamboozled

This chapter discusses the many reasons why church members are unwilling to confront the immoral behavior of church leaders. The reason is: they have been warned and falsely indoctrinated never to do so.

As discussed earlier, when Christian leaders are confronted on their lascivious behavior and/or false doctrine, hysterically, they attempt to turn the table on the whistleblower and accuse *them* of bad behavior; everything from being prideful, entertaining delusions, and being legalistic (that's church-speak for 'stiff 'n starchy').

"Now hold on just a minute," they'll protest. "Aren't you being just a little too legalistic right now?!"

In fact, don't be surprised if they stand up at the pulpit that next service and call the congregation to prayer about it.

"Ah yes, beloved, there's a legalistic spirit in the house tonight. We don't want that kind of thing here. Let's bind that evil spirit."

This happened to a friend of mine who lives up in Northern California. She attended a small, Pentecostal church and for a time, really enjoyed the services. Then, she happened upon one of their teaching DVDs touching upon 'purpose and predestination.'

On the DVD, the female minister spoke about the sexual abuse she suffered as a child, and the chaos it caused later in life. Then she dropped the bomb. Pulling a perfectly good scripture out of her hat, she bastardized its true meaning to make a foul allegation. Take a look:

Jeremiah 29:11: "For I know the thoughts that I think toward you; thoughts of peace and not of evil; to give you an expected end."

The minister used this passage to 'prove' that God predestined her molestation, as part of 'his plan' to prepare her for ministry. The allegation was outrageous! The woman alleged that God 'orchestrated' the rape against her when she was just a little girl, as part of his 'divine purpose' for her life.

This particular DVD actually ended up on worldwide, Christian television and no doubt bamboozled many others into believing that God 'designed' every hellish event that ever happened to them.

Now, my friend up in Northern California is well-versed in scripture and became unhinged by this creepy doctrine, so she wrote the senior pastor a polite email alerting him to the error, to which he replied:

"Well, the Apostle Paul said we see through a glass darkly."

This is more church-speak for, "We can't help it if we're ignorant." However, as ordained ministers, it is their responsibility to LEARN scripture and explain life's traumatic events CORRECTLY, not inadequately.

Lakevia Amey

How come both ministers had conveniently forgotten that Christ already identified who the true killer and destroyer is? Take a look:

John 10:10
The thief [Satan] comes only to steal, kill and destroy, but in me there is only life more abundantly.

James 1:16-17
Do not be deceived my beloved. Only good and perfect things come from the Father of Lights, in whom there is no variation or shadow of turning.

That next Sunday morning the pastor saw my well-versed friend, went to the pulpit and said:

"Ah yes, beloved, there's a legalistic spirit in the house today. We don't want that kind of thing here. Let's bind that spirit!"

Bamboozled

So my friend turned him over to the Lord (by prayer) for immediate correction. At the next service, the same pastor stood up, pointed a finger at my friend in front of the entire assembly and said, "Sister, there is a reason why you came to this city, and the Lord is about to fulfill all your purpose!" (More church-speak for 'Okay, so I guess we approve of you.')

At that moment, the pastor and my friend understood each other perfectly. He knew he had done wrong and was offering a token of peace, which my friend gladly received.

However, not all church leaders are so bright. Many insist on continuing to bamboozle the Body of Christ, especially in the Pentecostal sector. They regularly sprinkle their Sunday morning sermons with this next line of doctrine:

"The Lord said, 'Touch not my anointed!' You're not supposed to speak against the anointed of God! If you do, there will be a curse upon you!"

Well, this is true if the minister is not doing anything wrong; but if they are, this particular sermonette doesn't apply at all, nor is it scripturally correct.

When we take a closer look at the Old Testament incident which gave rise to this particular teaching, we find that God never said any such thing at all about corrupt ministers. David did! He is the one that said it, not God.

When David said this, he was referring to Saul; a man who had SINNED against God, was REJECTED by God, and was STRIPPED of the anointing. So, when David said this, there was no holy anointing left on Saul.

In the verse below, we can clearly see what God's true opinion was of Saul, and it ain't pretty.

1st Samuel 24:4

Then the men of David said to him, "This is the day of which the Lord said to you, 'Behold, I will deliver your enemy (Saul) into your hand, that you may do to him as you wish.'"

Clearly, God wanted the man dead. Notice that God identified Saul as the 'enemy' – not the anointed one. Notice also that God said he couldn't care less about what David did to him, up to and including killing him; and yet, the Pentecostal church persists.

As a result, Pentecostals continue to cite David's error as an excuse to cover up the immoral indiscretions of church leadership; but the truth is, Saul had become so depraved, it's a wonder that God hadn't killed him any sooner.

Saul suffered of manic depression brought on by his unrequited jealousy of David. When he slew Goliath, David was just a boy, and Saul couldn't take it. He was tormented day and night with jealousy because his own best warriors could not kill the giant. Then, along came this cheeky upstart with a sling-shot. It was enough to tip Saul right over the edge. Everyone knows that if we can't let go of something, it begins to erode the soul and cause many other mental-health problems. And this was the cause of Saul's demise.

Recall the many times when Saul's depression over-whelmed him and young David was called into his chambers to play the harp for him. Instead of allowing the Lord's anointed music to minister to him, Saul picked up a javelin on three separate occasions, hurled it at the boy, and attempted to pin him to the wall. (See 1st Samuel Chapter 18).

After that, David fled from the house of Saul and a decades-long, civil war broke out between the two sides. Over the next few years, God turned Saul over to David several times to be KILLED, but he refused to do it.

On the third occasion, Saul was crouching down in the bushes relieving himself, only a few feet away from David. Foolishly, David again refused to kill him because he was too afraid to do it. Instead, he kept saying, "I will not touch the Lord's anointed!"

In effect, David was like the children of Israel who refused to enter the Promised Land, and, like them, he chose to wonder about in the wilderness ten long years, rather than put Saul out of business. Because of David's error, many good lives were lost.

During one heart-breaking incident outlined in 1st Samuel Chapter 22, Saul murdered eighty-five of Israel's holiest priests, all innocent men with wives and children.

Suspecting them of hiding David, he lined them all up in a straight line and slaughtered them with the sword, one by one.

Touch not the 'anointed'? Well, that depends on what they're up to, doesn't it? David made a serious error when he said this and it controls much of the church's thinking today when it comes to confronting predators.

I have another friend who used to attend a well-known, Pentecostal church in Irvine, Orange County. The pastor there is a hot supporter of the 'Touch not my anointed' thing, and he seems to have sunken to new depths defending the vile doctrine.

As part of the membership process, new members are required to sit through classes and watch DVDs on various subjects, which my friend happily attended. However, some of the DVDs were particularly difficult to sit through. One covered the matter of 'Authority.'

On this DVD, the Irvine pastor taught a story that he actually shared many times from the pulpit, about a certain evangelical crusade he travelled with years earlier. The crusade's key speaker was a new, young evangelist who apparently packed out the house wherever he went. However, the young evangelist couldn't keep his hands to himself. Every night after the crusade, he picked up girls from the crowd and took them back to his hotel room.

The Irvine pastor said he and all the other ministers on the tour knew all about this, but they refused to say or do anything about it.

"Yes, we knew all about it, but the Lord said, 'Touch not my anointed!' No matter what sinful thing that evangelist did, we chose not to speak against him!"

the one with the gift of healing. All these people were getting healed, so the Lord was obviously using him, even though he was engaged in that sinful behavior!"

Little did he realize it was no longer the evangelist's gift in operation, but the Lord himself who took over the crusades. Many of these good people traveled from miles around to get there, so the Lord showed up FOR THEM; and not because of the man's so-called anointing.

Many in the church believe that spiritual gifts cannot be taken away because they are disbursed to us by God at birth. This is true, but there is nothing to stop us from abusing the gift and killing it. Later in the DVD, the

Irvine pastor also alleged that God will hurt, curse and sometimes kill people, if they ever dare to confront a minister on his behavior.

"Anyone who dares to speak against the anointed of God will be cursed! That's right; a curse will come upon them! Look at what happened to Miriam! She spoke against Moses and the Lord turned her into a leper!"

Then he quoted scripture after scripture to 'prove' the many ways God will curse someone for speaking against the anointed. However, the scriptures he quoted were all from the Old Testament. He conveniently failed to mention that all punishment was settled and paid in full through Christ on the cross.

The pastor also failed to mention that Miriam had accused Moses, turned people against him and almost started a riot for no good reason. He also failed to acknowledge these in-your-face tidbits:

Matthew 18:17(b)
And if he refuses to hear the offense, tell it to the whole church...

Lakevia Amey

1ˢᵗ Timothy 5:20-21
If any [minister] is sinning, rebuke him in front of everyone, so that all may fear. I charge you before God, Christ Jesus and the angels of God, to do this without prejudice and partiality.

1ˢᵗ Corinthians 5:11-13
But now I have written to you not to keep company with anyone named a brother, who is sexually immoral...Don't even eat with someone like that!

Okay, so which is it? Should we confront it, or keep our mouths shut? Around the same time that these DVDs were released, the Irvine church's membership shrank from over 2,000 to a paltry 200 in an unprecedented, overnight fashion. Could the DVDs be connected? There's a reason why so many churches remain small and of no consequence, and why some churches grow in health and prosperity.

Because of this vile teaching, many people at the Irvine church suffered unnecessarily. One incident involved a young, teenage girl, about sixteen years of age.

Bamboozled

She joined the Irvine church's youth group, which happened to be under the leadership of a certain, demented youth leader, who was in his late twenties.

One day, the youth leader made a pass at the teenage girl, which she rejected. As a result, he told the entire youth group, "She's a slut and from now on, I want everyone to stay away from her."

Needless to say, the teenage girl was humiliated and left the church. Now, her father was a police officer; a big block of a man. He told the Irvine pastor about this, and wanted to confront the youth leader himself, but the pastor forbade him to do so. He said:

"No, we can't do that. He is a minister of God and we cannot speak against him. We have to be obedient to the Lord, no matter what he did. Let's just pray for him."

My friend was present in class that day as the police officer told the whole story. He actually used the incident to teach 'obedience.' Instead of protecting his daughter, he was bamboozled into believing this false doctrine.

Later on the same DVD, the Irvine pastor taught on marriage; the authority of the husband and the wife's duty to submit. For the sake of illustration he invented a married couple. (Thankfully, they were not real people and he was speaking only hypothetically.)

In this scenario, the make-believe husband approaches his make-believe wife and says, "Honey, I would like for us to join a swingers' club and have sex with other people!"

The wife naturally becomes unglued and starts to cry and scream at her husband, and quote scripture about adultery. Next, the Irvine pastor can be seen on the DVD talking about the many ways the wife's behavior was 'ungodly.'

"She was very wrong to shout at her husband like that. A wife should never shout at her husband, no matter *what* he does!"

He seemed to have forgotten that, according to the Lord's own words, the husband had already committed adultery in his heart, and the wife was now free to file for divorce. Nevertheless, the Irvine pastor actually expected Christian women to act like *Sister Wives* at some FLDS compound.

Bamboozled

He continued, "The Apostle Paul said women should remain sweet and soft-spoken when they address their husbands, no matter what wrong the husband does. She was out of order!"

My friend kept waiting for the Irvine pastor to correct the husband for making that vile suggestion, but it never happened. He had no conception of the filth he was promulgating on that DVD. In effect, the husband had asked his wife to allow other men to rape her.

Think of it; she would have to strip naked, lay down, expose herself to the world, and allow other men to go into her. And she was wrong to complain?

What should have happened in this scenario is that the wife immediately calls the senior pastor of the church (provided she actually has a pastor in his right mind), whereupon the husband should be brought in for serious counseling and correction; preferably surrounded by several of the church's strongest and most foreboding men.

The DVDs in question have been circulated all over the world, to Australia and the U.K., and we are left to wonder if anyone in those churches had the good sense to reject those insane teachings.

James 3:1
Brothers, let not many of you become teachers, knowing we will receive the stricter judgment.

When ministers are exposed on their indiscretions, the church also likes to quote this oldie-but-goodie:

"Love covers a multitude of sins."

Okay, but that's the second part of the scripture. What about the first part? Let's look at the whole thing:

James 5:20
Let him know that, he who turns a sinner from the error of his ways, will save a soul from death and cover a multitude of sins.

Notice that we first have to TURN that person from their sin...THEN...we can cover it up. At the end of the day, we all have a responsibility to uphold the integrity of the Lord's word. Just because the church says something over and over, does not necessarily make it 'truth.' Below is a collection of responses that you can expect when confronting a church predator:

- Pride comes before a fall
- You're being legalistic
- Touch not the Lord's anointed
- Love covers a multitude of sins
- You're just imagining things

If you encounter any of the above, have ready the scriptures outlined in this chapter to counter the resistance at hand. You hardly have to say anything. Just let the scriptures do the talking. The bottom line is this: scripture on church immorality is final and cannot be argued with.

Chapter 7

The Sickroom

Church is a hospital full of sick people who are in need of some type of healing. After the kinds of events that you've read about so far, church should be a place where people can go to get delivered, healed, set free and get fed spiritual food by hearing the word of God.

The purpose of fellowship is to help build up the Body of Christ, not tear it down. Hebrews 10:25 encourages us never to forsake the assembling of the saints. Regretfully, I have yet another close friend to tell you about who fell victim to a church predator.

Like Sparkle, my other friend, Linda, was also in need of a church home. Linda was suffering of 'hurt disease.' Like me, she was hemorrhaging from the heart because she had been hurt so many times in years gone by, but she had the good sense to know that only Jesus, the doctor of her soul, could heal her. When Linda started attending a certain new church, she finally felt at home.

However, as soon as she started fellowshipping there, the men of the church began to pursue her. In fact, one of them was an ordained minister at the church. Here we go again.

The minister in question pursued Linda's affections for months on end before she ever went out with him. Once she did, they dated for eight happy months. In fact, they became so close, Linda introduced him to her family and friends, and they often met up for lunch during the week. Things were going well in the relationship and Linda was actually quite happy.

One day, I called her on the phone and asked if she ever prayed about this man, and she said no. I reminded her that before going out on dates, we should always pray first. I told her that believers are to pray about anything and everything. Sometimes we think that we know someone when really, we don't. God is the only one who knows the heart of a man and God is the only one that can reveal the heart of a man. He knows what's best for us.

After I got off the phone with her, I was lead to pray for her. A few days later I had a dream about her new beau. I saw him walk up to her front door and knock, but before she answered, he turned and walked away. Still in the dream, I saw him walking along on a clear, sunny day with an unknown woman on his right arm. Up ahead he saw my friend Linda, so he turned around and walked the other way with the unknown woman still on his arm.

When I woke up it was about three or four in the morning and I could not believe what I had seen in the dream. I grabbed my journal and started writing everything that I saw.

Later that morning, I drove to her house with the intention of telling her what I saw but when I got there, I declined to tell her because she seemed so happy. Everyone thought they made such a beautiful couple!

The ordained minister even discussed marriage with her! At the time, she did not have health benefits and he offered to put her on his plan once they got married. I often saw them together and this man in ministry seemed like such a nice person. So I stayed quiet but the dream was always in the back of my mind.

About two months after I had the dream, Linda's cousin ran into him at church and she happily asked him when they were going to get married. His response was mind-boggling.

"What are you talking about? We're just friends! I've already told her that I'm in a relationship with someone else!"

No actually, he never mentioned anything about this at all. Linda certainly did not know that he was in a relationship with another woman. In fact, the exact opposite was true. If he was, why did he spend so much time with Linda and her family? Apparently, he had deceived them all.

What he was trying to do here was totally obvious. It was his way of sending Linda the message by way of her cousin, that he was breaking up with her. He knew that

Linda's cousin would scurry off and tell her the news, sparing him the trouble of having to break it to her. He basically used Linda's cousin to do his dirty work, and Linda, of course, never saw it coming.

When Linda found out, she was heartbroken and humiliated. He and Linda had been dating a total of eight months. Come to find out, he met the other woman six months after he started dating Linda, which confirmed what I saw in the dream only two months earlier.

Later she told us that there was no way in the world that she would ever have spent a single day with that man, knowing he was in a serious relationship with another woman.

Because Linda believed that an ordained minister should not behave this way, she went to the pastor for counseling. During the session, he asked a most offensive question, as though to swat flies from the buttermilk.

"Well, did you ever kiss him?" Linda answered, "No," to which he replied, "Well, that means your relationship with him was not real. If you never even kissed, you were just friends!"

Why did this pastor not acknowledge the most obvious dysfunction here? Why would a man seriously involved with another woman spend oodles of time with Linda and her family? Then, the pastor said the most confounding thing.

"He also said that you knew about the other woman all along and that you were okay with that."

I could not believe my ears! That next Sunday, the pastor allowed the minister in question to stand at the pulpit and deliver a sermon. This was done to teach Linda a lesson and publicly humiliate her. It was pure evil at its very conception.

Linda was so upset by this betrayal she left the church. The minister, of course, stayed and acted as though he had done nothing wrong. And why shouldn't he stay there? He had become the pastor's darling while Linda was made the ugly duckling. He went on to marry the other woman and she never had a clue that during their entire 'happy engagement' her fiancé spent quality time with Linda.

The message in this story is that Linda was already sick when she came into 'the hospital.' She needed help and for months on end tried to keep herself pure from the cares of this world, and safe from yet another man who would hurt her. She was suffering from hurt disease. Her heart had been broken so many times in years past, she knew that no one could heal her but Jesus, the doctor of her soul. But this man came along and forced his way into her life with deceptive affections, and ruptured that healing work in progress. Then she had to start all over.

The purpose of her going to 'the hospital' (church) was to become well, not further sick. And while at 'the hospital' she caught yet another disease on top of the one she already had. The 'hurt disease' did not kill her. Complications arising from the hurt did.

When a patient has an already weak immune system, a virus such as pneumonia can take root and cause them to die. Linda died spiritually after this event because she had caught yet another disease that was too much for her to deal with.

She encountered two men who operated under the devil's lying spirit, and it caused her to stop breathing. She was never healed. This is what Satan does to us.

When he sees that God is about to bless us, he steps in to distract God's people with counterfeits and cheap facsimiles, in order to thwart the plan of God; sometimes permanently.

The minister whom Satan used operated totally from the flesh and there was no God in that man during the entire courtship. First, he was controlled by the lying spirit, and then a lustful spirit. Had he prayed to the Lord about Linda, he would have been warned to leave her alone because she was not ready to date. Had Linda prayed, the Lord would have also prevented the man from coming near her in the first place.

Matthew 12:31
Seek first his kingdom, and all these things
will be given to you as well.

When we go to church, we should first focus on things of God, get rooted and grounded in his word and allow him to minister to us. Seek after righteousness first and everything else will be added. No matter whom you date, at your church or another church, everything must be done in order and decency.

Also interesting to note is that the minister who pursued Linda, happened to be very good friends with the pastor who pursued Sparkle. Evil spirits will transfer from one body to the next.

When a pastor is out of order, the entire church is out of order. Birds of a feather flock together. This is what I call *Follow the Leader*...or...*Monkey See Monkey Do*. When leadership is corrupt, it will contaminate the entire flock.

> Matthew 12:1
> Meanwhile, when a crowd of many thousands had gathered, so that they were trampling on one another, Jesus began to speak first to his disciples, saying, "Be on your guard against the yeast of the Pharisees, which is hypocrisy."

Yeast is the biblical symbol for corruption. Its nature is to expand and spread corruption throughout the entire batch of bread-dough. One bad apple spoils the whole barrel. Jesus said hypocrisy can spread through one person, and contaminate the integrity of an entire church. At this writing, the minister in question has been married about six months to the other woman. Hence, the event is still fresh in everyone's mind. I recently spoke with Linda and she said that she ran into him at a restaurant. Ever since that day he started calling her on the phone. He had the nerve to ask Linda if they can continue to be friends and go out to lunch.

Why would a minister risk going out to lunch with a woman without the knowledge of his lawfully wedded wife? Why would a minister risk going to see other women after he successfully bamboozled his pastor into believing his innocence?

A married man's wife should be his very best friend. That is the way God designed it to be, and there is no other variation to that equation. This is the perfect example of how adultery gets started.

Technically, Linda could now set him up and prove to the pastor what an adulterous letch the man really is. In this day and age of video surveillance, predators like him are just not very smart.

Chapter 8

Fungus Feet

A lot of sin in the church is hidden, like fungus feet. Fungus mainly attacks the toenails and turns them into ugly, deformed crustaceans.

It's easy to hide fungus feet inside your socks and shoes. No one will ever know the condition of your toenails inside socks and you can blend in with people that have normal feet. No one will ever know.

You can put on a front for a long time, but eventually you have to take off your socks and shoes. In this case, the truth won't set you free; it will expose you. The truth is, you can only hide the fungus for so long.

In the meantime, it's easy to deceive others. Just lotion your feet really well and you can trick some of the people some of the time, but not all of the people all of the time.

Eventually you will run into someone who's already had fungus feet and can spot a cover up a mile away. In fact, having had the same problem, they know all the tricks to cover it up. Heck, they probably belong to a Fungus Foot Survivors' Group.

A woman with fungus feet can actually go to the nail salon and get her ugly crustaceans all dolled up. The nail shop will clip, buff, polish and decorate her fungi-toenails, and embellish them with sparkly flower designs and diamonds. The fungi-toenail-woman then leaves the salon happy, and goes out to buy a pair of strappy, high-heeled sandals.

Soon a man comes along and notices how pretty her feet look. He sits down next to her at the Starbuck's and compliments her on her pretty toes. In fact, he's quite bedazzled by all the sparkling trinkets and girlie-pink polish on her tootsies! Why, even Eddie Murphy in the film *Boomerang* would adore her lovely toes!

Fungus Feet

Little does he know, her feet are completely infected with fungus. If the man actually knew that her feet were infected, he would never have glanced her way. He would have taken off running down the street in the never-ending search of other sparkly toes.

No matter how much someone hides their fungi feet with pedicures, voluptuous shoes, sparkly trinkets and scented lotions, that person knows what's going on deep down inside. And so does the Lord.

Instead of turning to the Lord to cleanse their gangre-nous, awful-smelling feet, they will do anything and say anything to continue the deception, rather than allow their feet to be properly treated by a doctor. With this type of contamination you cannot go to just any doctor. It has to be a foot specialist, called a podiatrist.

Fungus is an aggressive, bacterial growth. In fact, you can watch it multiply under a microscope. If the feet are not properly treated, the fungus will not go away. It continues to spread and eventually takes over the entire foot. Fungus is also contagious and can infect others. What an industrious organism!

In order to heal the feet from the fungus, the infected person has to take internal medication to kill the fungus, or undergo expensive laser treatment.

Now, let's say the fungi represents sin; as in filth. We can hide sin all we like, but if the problem is not dealt with, it will eventually take over and become your god. If you deny treatment to that sick part of your being, your walk with Christ is completely contaminated. You cannot walk in Christ, laden with filth.

When church leaders continue without getting treated, their infections spread outward to their church members. We can deceive those who don't know better, but Christ knows the truth. We cannot deceive him or the people who are truly walking with Christ.

Proverbs 4:20-22
My son, attend to my words; incline your ear unto my sayings. Let them not depart from your eyes. Keep them in the midst of your heart, for my words are life to those that find them, and health to all their flesh.

Fungus Feet

The word of God, which is spirit and truth, is the only medication that can kill the fungus, and the only Doctor who can properly treat the fungus feet of the soul, is Christ Jesus. You have to have faith that the medication prescribed by the Great Physician, which is his word, will heal your feet. Repent, turn away from sin and your feet will be healed.

As Christians, we need to stop deceiving our brothers and sisters and walk in truth. Then you will be healed. Lies don't come from the Lord, and liars don't work for the Lord. They work for Satan because he is the father of all lies.

Satan is the opposite of Christ. Satan cannot tell the truth to save his own wretched, miserable life. He is a counterfeit, an imposter. He is also the creator of fungi feet.

Always remember that he was kicked out of Heaven because he desired to be God. There is only one God the Father, and there is only one Christ Jesus. All counterfeits are liars.

Chapter 9

She-Predator

A very beautiful young woman walked into our hair salon one day. She was so beautiful that all eyes were definitely on her. She looked as if she was mixed with perhaps two races, with a beautiful, glowing, olive complexion and long, dark hair with a natural sheen all its own. Her hair fell all the way down to her waist. She had come in that day to wait for her friend who was getting her hair done.

During our back and forth chatter, someone finally asked her if she was of a mixed race and she said, "No, I'm a pure Native American." How proud she was of her heritage as she responded with such boldness.

Lakevia Amey

As she waited for her friend to finish getting her hair styled, others asked the beautiful woman about her line of work. What did she do for a living? That's when her friend started to laugh.

She said, "Is the church still praying for you?" Now both of them laughed. No doubt it was an inside joke.

So, I turned and looked at the beautiful woman and asked, "Are you a Christian?" and she said, "Yes."

"So, why is the church praying for you?"

"They're praying for me to get delivered. They're also praying for God to bless me with a new job."

"Oh really? So what type of work do you do?"

"I'm a stripper!"

"Well, did you become a stripper before or after you became a Christian?" What a question. It was direct contradiction of terms.

She answered, "Before."

I asked if she wanted to be delivered, and she said, "No."

Then she told us the whole story. One day she was walking down the street and saw a man walking into a church whom she found to be very attractive. She walked passed the church a second time to get his attention as he stood in the parking lot of the church. They made eye-contact and then greeted one another. By then she knew that she pretty much had him wrapped around her little finger.

This is what predators do. They seek out what their flesh wants and then go after it. Notice also, that predators can be women whose agendas can many times be stronger than a man's. So she caught his eye and they started dating.

Shortly thereafter, she actually joined the church and received Christ as Lord and Savior, but kept her job at the strip club, where she stripped naked every night before hundreds of gawking men. She told us that she joined the church knowing that Christians want to get married, and are good providers. And it just so happened that she was looking for a financial benefactor.

When he found out that she was stripper, he wanted her to get delivered. At this point I asked her, "How in the world did you know that he would be attracted to you? Just because you're a beautiful woman doesn't mean that he was going to be attracted to you."

She laughed at this. The whole thing was a big joke to her. Because she was so utterly beautiful she knew that she could get him. Well, as you might have guessed, the man she met was a minister. How did a man of God end up with a stripper? Should we really continue to call him a 'man of God'? Isn't this just as contradictory as her line of work?

As she told us the story, she continued to laugh about the whole thing. The woman was a she-predator and was actually being used by Satan to bring down the man of God. Proverbs Chapter 6 warns that a harlot can bring the man down straight into the pit of hell.

Proverbs 6:24-28

To keep you from the evil woman, from the flattery of the tongue of a strange woman. Lust not after her beauty in your heart; neither let her take you with her eyelids. For by means of a whorish woman a man is brought to a piece of bread: and the adulteress will hunt for your precious life. Can a man take fire in his bosom, and his clothes not be burned? Can one go upon hot coals, and his feet not be burned?

She-Predator

What the minister didn't know is that the she-predator spotted her prey from a mile away and her intentions were to get him. She had no intention of getting to know Christ. And so the beautiful predator crept into his church. A man would definitely need the indwelling of the Holy Spirit to sniff this one out. Satan sends counterfeits to men and women of God to thwart them, drain them of strength and their anointing. It was the modern-day version of Samson and Delilah.

The Book of Judges Chapter 16 gives us an account of a woman named Delilah who used feminine allure to affect the destiny the man of God, named Samson; one of Israel's greatest judges. Delilah's story shows how men can be easily manipulated by women through their own desires.

Through her sexual attraction and cunning, she discovered the secret of Samson's immense, physical strength (it was in the length of his hair). The Lord instructed him never to reveal this to anyone, but he disclosed this to Delilah, and it proved to be fatal. When he finally revealed his secret, Delilah rushed over to the Philistine rulers to gather her reward and Samson was captured while asleep. His enemies gouged out his eyes and then strapped him to a millstone to tread like an animal for the rest of his natural life.

Samson didn't lose just his power. He foolishly stripped himself of his divine anointing. The result was, he lost his life and a whole city was destroyed.

This is what happens to Christian men. Many of them are so deceived they don't even know they're deceived!

Chapter 10

The Sofa Bandit

Around 2011, I was introduced to a minister at a church concert. We spoke in person a couple of times and eventually exchanged phone numbers. When we talked on the phone he was always gentle with me and never said anything out of order. How refreshing!

He often visited me at my church and we prayed together over the phone. After a few months he asked if he could take me out for lunch. There seems to be a pattern here. That day, he let me know that he was interested in dating me because I appeared to be "a hearer and doer of the word and practiced the fruits of the spirit." Then, he gave me his definition of dating.

He said the whole purpose of dating is to collect information, get to know one another, and should eventually lead to marriage. He said he was ready to get married and that he was not into spending time with me just to have fun. So far so good. During these conversations, he mentioned that he had two children, was laid off from work and was expecting to receive a call to go back to work any day. He was also blind in one eye which apparently occurred as a result of some childhood trauma at the hands of his mother.

I appreciated the fact that he was being up front and honest with me. I told him that we can continue to talk on the phone and have prayer, but I did not think it was a good idea to go out on dates until we heard from the Lord. As a result, we decided to fast and pray about the situation.

It makes no sense to me to become attached to someone if we are not called to be married, and I don't believe in going out to dinner just to receive free meals, kill the boredom, or have something 'lined up' for Saturday night.

The Sofa Bandit

When I'm going out with someone, I care about what they feel. Just because two Christians of the opposite sex are congenial and appear to practice the fruits of the Holy Spirit, does not mean they are meant for one another. I told him that I personally think when Christians start dating seriously without hearing from the Lord, this opens doors for heartbreak. Why? Because once a man and woman become attached, it will be very difficult to part. What if the Holy Spirit says 'no'? Separating will cause a lot of unwanted pain.

The problem is, most Christians will probably allow themselves to be ruled by the flesh (emotions) and ignore the Holy Spirit. However, true love is not based on emotions. This is how Satan creeps in. He entraps us through the pain of our own, wanton emotions. For this reason, it is so important not to make decisions based on emotions.

Two weeks after I told this man that we should wait to hear from the Lord, I had a vision. I was sitting in a van filled with brides, and we were being prepared for marriage. Each bride had to undergo a process. Still in the vision, the brides and I stood in a horizontal line wearing wedding gowns. Our dresses started out as the color off-white and slowly turned a bright, glowing snow-white. Then, we found ourselves back in the van and were dropped off at a corner. We had to walk across the street to a chapel, and stand in line once again.

At the chapel, the door opened and we were presented to our husbands. Still in the vision, I noticed that my dress had not turned completely snow-white. It was very close to it, but not quite. Its color was just one shade lower than snow-white.

My turn came up to step out of the van and walk up to the chapel. As I tried to do so, I was told not to, but I tried to go inside the chapel, anyway. I was convinced that my dress was white enough, so I stepped out of the van.

All the other brides had on snow-white dresses, and when they were presented to their husbands, they got married and walked off with one another. When it was my turn to be presented to my husband, the door shut, and never opened again. I stood there waiting. I was never presented to my husband and I ended up walking to the bus stop all alone, waiting for my husband to arrive.

That's when I realized the Holy Spirit was answering my prayer concerning the man I was becoming involved with. I called him on the phone and told him what the Lord showed me. Refreshingly, he received what I told him, and we continued to pray and fellowship occasionally over the phone.

Now, because he was unemployed, his financial condition had worsened considerably. In fact, by this time he was basically living out of his car. Then, I received a phone call from my mother and she asked if I knew anyone looking for work at the time, because Ralph's Supermarket was hiring.

I called the man right away to tell him about the great job opportunity but he said he didn't want to fill out an application. He didn't like grocery store hours.

I would think that a person who doesn't have a place to sleep would jump on the opportunity to fill out an application; especially if they are in the process of becoming homeless, not to mention desiring to get married. A week later, he called and said that his car had been impounded and he needed $300 to get the car out of impound. He had parked it in a red zone.

If the car was the mainstay of his life, why would he park it so recklessly? Readers, I don't know about you but that sounds like a personal problem. It was not up to me to get his car out of impound. How was he going to pay me back? It's impossible to pay someone back when you don't have a job.

I did offer to take him to the impound to get all of his belongings out of his car. Because he didn't have the money to get the car out of impound, he was definitely going to lose it. When we arrived at the lot to retrieve his belongings, I noticed that everything he owned was inside that car.

Two weeks later he called again. This time he had misplaced his unemployment papers. This was a man who needed to get his act together and take responsibility over his actions. Failing to get our act together and take responsibility over our lives can lock us out, not only of heaven, but can ruin our inheritance here on Earth!

After it all fell apart, I said, "Thank you, Jesus, for showing me that he was not my husband."

The Sofa Bandit

Before long he was completely destitute and had no place to go. His ex-wife offered to let him sleep on her couch until he was able to find another place to stay. He also asked his pastor if he could stay at the church and the pastor said 'no.' Apparently, the pastor tried helping someone once before and could spot a repeat dead-beat a mile away. His pastor did, however, advise him to be very careful about moving in with his ex-wife. When he moved into her place, she treated him very badly and I felt sorry for him.

We would talk on the phone and I could hear her in the background calling him every name in the book but the child of God. When he received his unemployment check, he gave her $200.00 dollars. She took the money and put him out on the street.

Then, his ex-mother-in-law took pity and invited him to stay with her. I didn't hear from him for a month and finally he called me. During this conversation, he said that he had run into an old flame. One would think that by now, after all the chaos he suffered, he might have tried to get his personal life together; but his main focus was still on marriage, as though the Lord would present him with a bride in this current, broken condition!

I argued, "Wait a minute! You just got out of a divorce! You need to heal up because you have an open wound. If you don't stop you will get attacked by a shark!"

I continued, "You don't need to get caught up in a rebound relationship because you're going to end up getting hurt. Besides you have no money, no job and no place to live!"

I pointed out that it would be very difficult for a woman to respect him as the head of the household because of his situation. I also wondered how long it would take his wife to notice the reckless manner in which he conducted all the affairs of his life.

I said, "Don't get me wrong; I am not trying to put you down. I'm just trying to give you sound advice from a woman's point of view." He didn't respond and actually listened to me. "If you get married now you will give the woman the upper hand, and reverse rolls with her. The marriage will start out tolerable at first, and your flesh might be satisfied for a minute or two."

I went on to tell him that the woman in question will marry him, if she is desperate enough. "But once she realizes that you're not capable of contributing to the household, the honeymoon will soon be over. She'll end up resenting you, and that's when it leads to verbal abuse and rebellion."

The scenario I described for him is one that plays out in many households around America. That is why so many women are angry, make wrong decisions and settle for less. Desperate women deceive themselves by saying it's all right to settle for a dysfunctional man. To them it doesn't matter if he doesn't have a job and fails to contribute to the household.

In fact, many women will do and say anything they can (like those guests on the Jerry Springer Show) to hold onto their dysfunctional men. They've got it in their heads that they can't get anything better. They are trapped in the vicious cycle of the shattered self-esteem. Women also rationalize the dead-beat existence of their men.

"Well, he can stay at home and be Mr. Mom," they'll say. "We can save money on child care expenses!"

Eventually her friends notice things and express the obvious. "What? He doesn't have a car?"

"That's okay," she rationalizes. "He can drop me off at work and have access to the car during the day."

"So who pays the utility bills and buys the food and gas?"

"Well, I do for now, but that's just until he gets back on his feet!"

Sooner or later it all falls apart. He'll crash the car or meet someone younger and prettier. Players like that know how to work women. Or, the working woman gets burned out on having to be the sole bread-winner and eventually feels she deserves better. Baby woke up.

So, there we were talking on the phone and I actually thought he was listening to my advice, but it went in one ear and out the other. He had become a professional Sofa Bandit.

I guess he didn't like the advice that only a true friend would give. Sometimes the truth hurts but it helps us in the long run if we face it and implement change before it's too late. After that I didn't talk to him for two months. Eventually, he ran into one of my fellow church members and told him that he would soon be getting married. When I called, he answered the phone and said:

"I'm in Vegas about to get married as we speak!"

I said, "Are you crazy? Why did you answer the phone?"

His response was, "Oh, I'm waiting for the bride to walk down the stairs."

He was very excited so I said, "Well, go ahead and get married. Enjoy the rest of your day, enjoy the honeymoon and tell the bride that I said congratulations."

He called me a week later and I said, "Well, I guess God did send your old flame back for a reason."

He laughed and responded, "She's not my old flame. She is someone new."

That's when I started laughing uncontrollably. This is the same man who thought I was to be his wife only two short months ago.

"So, where did you meet this new woman?"

He became defensive and said, "Well, first, you should know that this marriage is ordained by God."

I said, "Okay, Mr. Ordained-By-God, where did you meet?"

"On a Christian internet dating site."

I said, "Oh, okay; well I thought about signing up on one of those sites before, but how do we know that the person is really a Christian? I have always felt like Christian dating sites are not very reliable because everyone knows that Christians want to get married, so they prey on Christians on these websites."

He replied, "And that's exactly what happened to me."

He went on to say that his wife was not saved when they first met on the site. Wait a minute! Didn't he just say "the marriage was ordained by God"? I continued to listen.

He told her that he wanted a saved, sanctified and Spirit-filled wife and stopped all communication with her. Then she contacted him a few weeks later to inform him that she had received Christ and they started talking again.

"We dated a long time..."

I interrupted him and argued, "Wait a minute! You just told me that you had known her for only a month before you got married."

The Sofa Bandit

He explained, "Well, when you talk to someone every day it feels like you have known them for a life time."

I conceded that this was possible, having experienced this myself. However, his story got nuttier by the minute. Throughout their so-called long courtship, he lived in Los Angeles, while she was in Las Vegas, and they never met in person until the day of their wedding! And it was ordained by God; right?

Right after the wedding he came back to California and...that's right, you guessed it...slept on his mother-in-law's sofa. The good news was, if only for the moment, he moved to Las Vegas to live with his new wife and was able to find work.

Whenever we move in a direction without the Holy Spirit, we place ourselves in the danger zone, where the enemy has the legal right, if you will, to attack us any way he likes. About five months later, I ran into his ex-sister-in-law and asked how he was doing.

She said, "Girl, what do you mean how is he *doing?* He's miserable and is going through a ton of stuff. The woman he's married to now is verbally and physically abusive towards him!"

Lakevia Amey

Didn't I tell him this was going to happen? He didn't want to listen. Women have certain principles and expectations of men that were placed there by God. Saved or not, we all have expectations; but he was so desperate to get married, he allowed himself to become an open target for a predator. Or, was his love-affair with the sofa too much for his new wife to deal with?

Chapter 11

The Jezebel

Once upon a time, a young man got dressed and went out to a nightclub. This young man grew up in church and was by that time happily backslidden. In fact, he wanted nothing to do with church or church people. Having grown up in a so-called Christian home, he had his fill of hypocrisy and deception.

At the club he met a beautiful woman and asked her to dance. Her name was Jezebel.

After the club closed down, Jezebel took the young man to her home for a night cap, as it were. Naturally, one thing led to another and they ended up in the bedroom. Jezebel kept the man locked in her bedroom for seven days and seven nights, and he was more than happy to be imprisoned in her sheets and sweaty perfumes. On the seventh day, Jezebel dropped the bomb. She said, "I'm a Christian."

Incredulous, he responded, "What? Well, why didn't you mention that before we got jiggy with it?"

Piously, she replied, "As a Christian woman, I'm not supposed to have sex. I'm saving my body for the Lord."

Then she said, "If you want to continue this relationship we will need to get married."

The Jezebel had manipulated him with an appetizer, of things to come, and he, blind to the wiles of this demon, gave in to her wishes. They went out and got married. However, the appetizer that Jezebel fed the man before they got married happened to be a whole lot better than the bowl of gruel he got after they tied the knot. He started attending church with her and noticed she was one way in front of her church friends, and completely different at home.

In fact, with the little knowledge that he had of scripture, he finally realized that the Jezebel didn't line up with scripture at all, once she set her foot outside the church. I ran into the young man years later, whereupon he admitted that living with her was like living with Satan.

Women of God, if you find yourself manipulating someone into marrying you, please note that you are totally out of the will of God. Manipulation is a form of witchcraft.

That's right, you don't have to wear a black hat, fly on a broom and mix potions in a bubbling pot to engage in witchcraft. You can perform witchcraft just by purposely obstructing the will the God or forcing your will upon others.

The Apostle Paul instructed that no one in the Body of Christ should deceive and take advantage of other Christians, make direct reference to 'personal affairs.' He gave us three areas in life where sanctification should take place:

1. The Marriage Relationship:

Sexual purity cannot be compromised. Sexual intimacy is for married couples only.

2. Brotherly Love Among the Brethren:

As Christians we should be able to love and trust one another inside the church.

3. The Church:

We must do everything in order and decency, according to the instructions of God.

> 1 Thessalonians 4: 3-8
> It is God's will that you should be sanctified and avoid sexual immorality; that each of you should learn to control his own body in a way that is holy and honorable; not in passionate lust like the heathen who do not know God; and that in this matter, no one should wrong his [brother or sister] and take advantage of them. The Lord will punish men for all such sin, as we have already told you and warned you. For God did not call us to be impure, but to live a holy life. Therefore, he who rejects this instruction does not reject man but God...

The Jezebel

Believers cannot afford to live double lives and think they can serve both God and the devil. His principles will win the respect of those outside of church and set us apart as the Lord's own people. And yet the church is filled with predators and Jezebels.

The Jezebel is a controlling spirit. The Lord spoke openly against this evil spirit in the Book of Revelations, therefore, persons operating under this spirit might want to be very careful. Take a look:

Revelations 2:20-23
Nevertheless I have a few things against you, because you allow that woman Jezebel, who calls herself a prophetess, to teach and seduce my servants to commit sexual immorality and eat things sacrificed to idols. I gave her time to repent of her sexual immorality, and she did not. Indeed I will cast her onto a sickbed, and those who commit adultery with her into great tribulation, unless they repent of their deeds. I will kill her children with death, and all the churches shall know that I am He who searches the minds and hearts. And I will give to each one of you according to your works.

Jezebel is not only an evil spirit, but she was also a queen of Israel who promoted the immoral cult of Baal. Her name is used in Revelations Chapter 2 to identify a false teacher; a so-called prophetess who misled believers.

In prior chapters we discussed men and women who lied, deceived and manipulated members of the Body of Christ in flagrant disregard of the Lord's warnings. They are, in fact, in grave danger of damnation because the Lord said, "If you have done these things to the least of these, you have done it to Me." He also said, "When the master of the house returns and finds that evil servant abusing others, He will tear that one in two."

The consequences for those operating under the influence of the Jezebel are absolutely blood-curdling. Still want to deceive and manipulate?

The Jezebel deceives its servants into thinking that it is perfectly acceptable to lie, cheat, deceive, and manipulate others, as though there is no consequence at all. Too many Christians practice the witchcraft of manipulation. We can talk about the Harry Potter movies all we want, but the same thing is going on in the Body of Christ. I am writing to inform you that Christ is not pleased with the actions of a lot of believers. They should be reminded to repent and turn away from sin, not coddle and cover it up, and yet that is exactly what Satan wants us to do...cover it up and never speak of it. That way, the sins may continue to multiply and writhe like insect larvae. Christ died for us to live in holiness and new life, not for us to hurt, manipulate, and deceive others.

> 1st John 2:3-6
> We know that we have come to know him if we obey his commands. The man who says: I know him, but does not do what he commands is a liar and the truth is not in him. But if anyone obeys his word, God's love is truly made complete in him. This is how we know we are in him. Whoever claims to live in him must walk as Jesus did.

That's a tall order that many of us may never achieve, but the Lord does not grade on achievement. He grades on EFFORT. He look for 'spirit and truth'.

Chapter 12

The Divine
Intervention of
Ms. Stephanie Smith

Let's now move the heart-warming story of Stephanie Smith. It's a story of new life, rescue and redemption; the way things ought to be in the Body of Christ.

It's a well-known fact, especially in the secular fields of psychology and law enforcement, that the abused can often become the abuser. Abuse is a learned behavior passed down from generation to generation. Many times it's so deeply rooted in the human psyche, it seems to dominate one's very DNA.

That is why, for example, there is no known cure for pedophilia, except through a direct intervention from Christ Himself.

Now, just because someone has been abused does not necessarily mean they will automatically become an abuser. Please don't allow yourself to become a predator just because someone preyed on you. Getting even is not the solution to the problem.

The bottom line is, if you become a predator it will commence a domino effect that leads to others getting hurt, while you continue to stay in bondage.

The injuries sustained from abuse are much more serious than you think. They can become self-inflicted wounds that cause greater anguish than the initial wound. Those who survived abuse are often traumatized by the constant pain of the open wound.

I met a young, Christian woman at my former place of work. For the purpose of this chapter, let's call her Stephanie Smith.

Stephanie was the victim of many predators, starting with her stepfather, who molested her as a young child, and yet she was raised in the church.

The Divine Intervention of Ms. Stephanie Smith

Once she left home, Stephanie naturally wound up in the viscous cycle of the questionable lifestyle. She ended up pregnant at a very young age, and became a single mother. Her son's father and every boyfriend after that did nothing but take advantage of her. Like so many other girls of her sad background, Stephanie continued to search for love in all of the wrong places. Before long, any semblance of the Lord in her life, had fully disintegrated down to nothing.

Stephanie could never find anyone to depend on or lean on. In each relationship she wound up as the sole breadwinner of the household again and again, and all the burdens fell on her.

When I met Stephanie, she was working a low-paying job which was barely enough for her to make ends meet. Therefore, she took on a second job. Two weeks after she started the second job, she met a gentleman who claimed to be a Christian. By now, Stephanie was accustomed to meeting men who were unemployed, so when this young man asked her out on a date, she was overwhelmed.

She said, "Lakevia, I finally met a real man and he's a Christian. He attends college, and has a car!" This was significant because all the guys she was ever involved with were such losers, they never had transportation of their own.

And so, the Christian man took her out on a date. When she came to work the next day she was so excited.

I asked, "Were did you go?"

Bright-eyed she said, "We had such a good time. He asked me what restaurant I wanted to go to. He said we could go wherever I want, so we went to the Subway."

Astounded by this, I said, "Are you crazy?"

Having never experienced the pleasant things in life, Stephanie's expectations were painfully low.

As a result, to Stephanie the Subway Sandwich shop must have seemed like the Beverly Wilshire. So I clued her in.

"Any time a real man asks you to choose a restaurant, he is talking about a real restaurant, like a nice steak house, not Subway! Even Home Town Buffet or the Sizzler are considered low-class for a first time date, but that would have been a lot better than Subway!"

She explained, "Well, he bought me a combo meal and also got one for me to take home to my son!" She acted as though she won the lottery.

I tried to explain to Stephanie that by setting such low standards, she may have given this man the wrong impression. Would he now treat her less, because she expected less?

"The next time he takes you out, he's probably going to treat you like a $5.00 Foot Long Special. You basically told him in so many words that you're not used to having nice things."

The next time they went out, he did exactly what I predicted. He took her to a fast food joint, and bought her something off the 99 cent menu. Then he drove her to his friend's house and tried to talk her into having sex. But Stephanie was a smart girl that night. She did not sleep with him and made him take her home. When Stephanie came to work the next day, she was really upset about the so-called gentleman's behavior.

"I'm tired of meeting liars. I've been practicing celibacy for several years and I'm trying my best to live right. But now I'm starting to deprive myself just to follow Christ. I want to go to a nightclub. I haven't been to one for so long."

Satan had targeted her for destruction. He knew she would not give in to fornication, but he knew that he could disintegrate her resolve and make her lose heart. By crumbling her heart, he could entrap her back into the former lifestyle.

Then she asked a pointed question. "I don't understand why Christians can't go to a nightclub." She was understandably speaking from weariness and loneliness. Roman 14:16 encourages us to the set the record straight on all things that are confusing. The Apostle Paul said, "Do not allow what you consider good, to be spoken of as evil."

I explained to Stephanie that the Bible does not say believers cannot go to a nightclub, but as saints of the Most High God, we have been called out of the world and sanctified, which means set apart. I explained that, whereas we can go anywhere in the world that we want to, it may not be the healthiest choice for us.

Nightclubs, for instance, can lead believers into sin if they are weak. Furthermore, if a believer is spiritually strong they probably would not consider going in the first place. As we discovered in the last chapter, nightclubs are the hunting ground of predators and Jezebels, so should we really walk into their territory?

Still ministering to Stephanie, I said, "I can't tell you what to do, but I know that you know better. You can deceive yourself if you want to. Pray about it and the Lord will tell you what to do."

Next thing I knew, Stephanie went to the unsaved co-workers to seek their advice. 2nd Timothy 4:3 states, "For the time will come when men will not put up with sound doctrine. Instead, to suit their own desires, they will gather around them a great number of teachers to say what their itching ears want to hear."

Without God's wisdom it's very easy to hear whatever will foster our own self-interest. A good example of this is King Ahab whose activities are recorded in the 1st Book of Kings. Ahab wanted the prophets to tell him only what he wanted to hear, whether it was the truth or not. People with itchy ears oppose sound doctrine because it doesn't line up with the gospel of their own selfish desires. That day, the unsaved co-workers told Stephanie what she wanted to hear.

"Girl, you know the Bible doesn't say you can't go to the club. Christians need to stop with that mess. You need to go out and have a good time!"

I was not led to say anything else to her after that. I often gave her rides home because she had no transportation. That night on the way home she said, "I'm tired of being used. I'm about to reverse the roles and start treating men the way they treat women. I'm going to start using them to get whatever I can get out of them."

I listened to her as she spoke because I realized that she was hurting and needed someone to talk to. I started praying for her. What I love about prayer is that you don't have to get permission from someone to pray for them. Just pray if that's what the Spirit leads you to do. This time, instead of taking her home she asked me drop her off at the dress shop up the street. Stephanie was going to buy an outfit to go to the club that night.

It took me about 15 minutes to make it home on the freeway. When I got home I prayed for her again. When I finished praying my phone rung and it was Stephanie.

She said, "Lakevia, you will never guess what happened. When you dropped me off at the store, just as I started walking in, two men came up behind me, and one of the guys yelled out, 'Excuse me miss!' I didn't turn around because I thought he was trying to flirt with me, so he yelled out again, 'Excuse me miss!' That time I turned around and there was this young man standing there. He said, 'Miss, I don't know anything about you or where you're going, but the Holy Spirit told me to tell you not to go where you are planning to go tonight, because you will not make it out alive.' Then he said, 'Can I pray for you?'"

The young man gave her some scriptures to read, and invited her to his home church. She thanked him and he began to glorify God on the street.

"All glory be to God. I don't know you. All I did was deliver the message that God told me to give to you."

I said, "Praise God!" and I meant it with all my heart.

So I told Stephanie that I prayed for her while we were in the car and also when I got home.

"I was not led to say anything else to you about nightclubs because you were not going to receive anything from me, anyway. Warning comes before destruction. That's what the Lord did for you."

Stephanie continued, "The young man actually said I would not have left there alive. There is no telling what would have happened to me. Someone probably would have tried to kill me."

I was led to tell her that it didn't necessarily mean physical death. It could also could have meant spiritual death and a complete separation from God. Who knows, she may have met yet another abusive man at that night-club, who would eventually take her life a year down the road. This particular event took place on a Friday after work. When I arrived at work on Monday, Stephanie had another testimony to share with me.

"When I went to church on Sunday morning, the first lady told me that she had a dream about me, and she needed to speak to me after church."

The first lady said, "The Lord showed a vision of you. In the vision, you were doing a lot of talking. You were running your mouth 100 miles per hour. You would not listen to anyone, and you were about to prostitute your-self."

The Divine Intervention of Ms. Stephanie Smith

Stephanie was astounded. Only the Lord could have shown this to the first lady and she knew exactly what she meant. Stephanie explained that as she prepared to come to work on Friday morning, she stood in front of the mirror and began to tell herself how much she didn't need a man.

"I'm tired of being lied to and manipulated by men," she said out loud into the mirror. It's time for me to start treating them the way they treat me! I'm going to have sex with them without any emotional ties, and I'm only gonna' go after men with money. I'm gonna' beat that money out of them!"

Stephanie was about to become a prostitute without ever realizing it. Trying to get even would not only lead her to hurt others, but she would have caused herself more pain in the long-run, resulting in physical or spiritual death.

Roman 12:17 warns, "Do not repay evil for evil." Be careful to do what is right in the eyes of everyone and mostly before God. Ladies and gentlemen, you don't have to stand on a street corner, work as a call girl or escort service to be a prostitute. A lot of men and women are prostituting themselves and don't even realize it. This kind of activity occurs every day out in the world and now seems to be creeping into the church. Or has it always been there?

It's a problem that needs to be dealt with. We serve a God so full of grace and mercy. He loves us so much. He doesn't want us to fall or get hurt. Hence, he will always send his children a warning to let them know trouble is just around the corner.

On the following page is an example of Israel's unfaithfulness to God. The Hebrew language uses words like 'spirit' to describe a person's inner character and disposition. Israel's tendency, during the centuries after Solomon, was to commit spiritual prostitution by being unfaithful to God by chasing other gods, in the same way that a prostitute solicits customers to buy sexual favors.

Since the worship of foreign gods frequently involved literal prostitution, in the following passage we see that the Israelites had become dangerously involved in this practice. Today people can be tempted to be unfaithful toward God by abandoning their commitment to him.

Hosea 4: 12-14

My people consult a wooden idol and are answered by a stick of wood. A spirit of prostitution leads them astray; they are unfaithful to God. They sacrifice on the mountaintops and burn offerings on the hills, under oak, poplar and terebinth trees where the shade is pleasant. Therefore your daughters turn to prostitution and your daughters-in-law to adultery. I will not punish your daughters when they turn to prostitution nor your daughters-in-law when they commit adultery, because the men themselves consort with harlots and sacrifice with shrine prostitutes; they are a people without understanding that come to ruin.

Many Christians do not believe that it is possible to walk in the office of a prophet, or that God communicates with his people through a vision. However, visions are supernatural revelations, messages and insights communicated through images seen within a person's mind or spirit. The pictures seen in the vision illustrate current events, spiritual truths or future events (Isaiah 1:1).

In the case of Stephanie, the Lord sent a messenger with a warning. We know it was from the Lord because Satan does not send prophets to do God's work. Had the messenger not come for Stephanie that day at the dress shop, and had the first lady not told her about the vision, Stephanie would have self-destructed.

The word of God states in 2nd Peter 3:9, "The Lord is not slow in keeping his promise, as some understand slowness. He is patient with us; not wanting anyone to perish but everyone to come to repentance."

When Stephanie was confronted with how much God loves her, I'm happy to announce that she repented that day and follows Christ even at this writing. God is using her as a powerful spoken-word artist who ministers to women and helps them come out of bondage. Glory to God in the highest for what he did. It was the divine intervention of Ms. Stephanie Smith.

Chapter 13

So Over the world

I remember one night when the Lord appeared to me in a dream. He met me right where I was, in my present, spiritual condition. I remember him saying to me, "I'm going to take you out of this world."

I wanted to go with him but didn't want to leave everything behind, especially my family. So, I started crying because I wasn't quite ready to let go of everything so familiar to me.

Still in the dream, the Lord lifted me up into the air. He held out his hand for me to leave the world and follow him. As I got closer to him, I felt so much power emitting from his person, I was afraid to look at him.

I turned my head to the side to deflect from his power, and reached out for his hand. As I reached out, I suddenly doubted that he was really the Christ. Our hands almost touched, but right before he grabbed my hand, I said, "I'm not ready."

And then he disappeared. The Lord left me in this world I suppose because I had made that choice, but I could not understand why he wanted to take me out of the world so soon.

Two years later, I was driving down the street and I was suddenly reminded of the dream. The car radio was on and I listened to the lyrics of the songs that came on. I could not believe what I was hearing. Every song was all about sex, booty-popping, getting all the girls you can get, and violence. I mean, every song was totally contrary to the Lord and I couldn't take it anymore. So, I cut off the radio and went to Wal-Mart that day, bought Gospel music and have been listening to the Lord's music ever since.

Later that night I watched TV but every station was saturated with witchcraft, violence, greed, sadism and all things that erode the soul. It was as though I had become intensely sensitive that day to anything and everything that did not line up with the Lord. And that's when it hit me.

Two years earlier, the Lord told me he was about to take me out of the world. He wasn't saying that he was going to physically take me out. I thought he meant I was going to die, and would never be able to see my family, at least not until the Lord's Return. I remember thinking, I'm too young to die, and I haven't gotten to the fun stuff. In my limited understanding back then, I believed that going to heaven meant 'death' when in fact it meant life everlasting, in a place far more alive than this.

With this encounter, the Lord was not telling me to die the physical death, but to die to my own self and follow him. In so many words, I was afraid to leave behind my old ways, my clothing, my home and my possessions. Little did I know that Christ had a plan for my life. And that plan was for me to serve him and no longer be a servant to the world. He was basically calling me out of the darkness into his marvelous light.

Back then, I had no idea that it was much better to live for Christ than to live for the world. Believers often have a problem with shedding bad habits that they learned in the world. It is impossible to follow Christ and hold onto the worldly ways of life. We have to die to those bad habits or they will become our god. Remember, anything that you love more than God is your god.

It's not easy letting go of habits. We all have habits that are hard to shake off. In fact, we already know that a lot of our bad habits are not healthy nor worth holding on to. After doing something for so long it becomes a part of us and can actually consume us, but that doesn't mean it's right for you.

Sometimes it's frightening when we make changes in our lives, but remember godly changes are only meant to make you a better person. Matthew 6:24 states, "No man can serve two masters: for either he will hate the one and love the other; or else he will hold to the one, and despise the other. You cannot serve God and mammon."

Spiritual double-vision causes one to believe he can serve two masters. Total loyalty to God cannot be divided between Him, and one's material possessions.

A master is a lord or an owner. God claims total lordship over his people, therefore, Jesus rightly proclaimed, "You cannot serve God and mammon."

1 John 2; 15 – 17

Do not love the world or anything in the world. If anyone loves the world, the love of the father is not in him. For everything in the cravings of sinful man, the lust of his eyes and the boasting of what he has and does, come not from the father but from this world. The world and its desires pass away, but the man who does the will of God lives forever.

According to the verse above, God loves his creation and the people who are in it, but he lets us know that God hates worldly ways. Therefore, we should never love the sinful ways of the world.

It is very difficult for a man to overcome the world on his own. It is the power of the Holy Spirit that gives us the ability to overcome the world.

Lakevia Amey

When I was a little girl, one of my favorite music artists was Prince and my favorite song was *I Will Die 4 U* Whenever I have private worship time with the Lord, he would always put that song in my heart. The problem is, why would he put a Prince song in my heart? I didn't understand. It got to the point to where I could actually hear the song in the head, clear as day, and feel the dance step that went along with that song.

This is significant because I cannot dance. I've never had rhythm and was never a dancer. In fact, I used to pray and ask God to teach me how to dance. When I was younger, I wanted to learn the *Drop It Like It's Hot* dance, and all those other cool steps but it never happened. I don't even know how to do the electric slide.

So, don't invite me to your next party if you expect me to get up and dance. We should also stop believing the world's old sayings that don't line up with scripture, such as: all African Americans have rhythm and soul. Believe me, I do not fit that description. This is why no family member or friend has ever seen me dance, because I can't do it!

Later in life, I wanted to learn how to dance so that I could go to the club and 'shake my tail feather' like everyone else, but that never happened either. In fact, I learned how to clap and stomp my feet at the same time only just recently! How funny! Go ahead, laugh out loud; the joke is on me!

And then along came that song by Prince. Whenever I heard that song, for the first time in my life, I felt rhythm and cadence. My feet and arms moved in perfect time to every note of the song.

When Prince performed *I Will Die 4 U* he danced his steps and then at the word 'U' he pointed to the audience in perfect rhythm. When I danced to that song, I found a new rhythm and dance, and pointed to heaven.

Throughout my life, I would sing and dance to that song in my hurt and in my darkest hour, and before long I realized the Holy Spirit had not only given me a new song, but a new praise dance in my heart.

Now Philippians 4:13 does promise that I can do everything through him, who gives me strength. In other words, I can do all positive things that Christ desires for me to do. This is significant because I've always thought it was impossible to turn my back on the world and leave it. Christ gave me the power and ability to accomplish what he wanted me to do, and he wanted me to be content in him and do his will.

Again, back when I was a little girl, one of my favorite cartoons was Popeye. Ha ha! Popeye consisted of three main characters: Popeye the sailor man, Brutus, and Olive Oyl.

Popeye was a puny, little man, who I believe suffered from 'short-man syndrome.' But Brutus was a large man who often bullied Popeye, and they competed constantly over the affections of Olive Oyl.

What I love about this cartoon is that whenever Popeye tore open a can of spinach and shoved it into his mouth, he became powerful; so powerful that he could punch out Brutus with his little finger! When Brutus saw Popeye coming after he ate the spinach, he already knew that he was defeated and took off running. Once he ate that spinach, Popeye was able to conquer all obstacles. Although Popeye was small in size, he had a lot of power after consuming the spinach. There are a lot of similarities in this cartoon between God and man.

Popeye represents man. The can of spinach represents the Holy Spirit. Brutus represents the devil, who will run all over us if we allow him to. But once we get pumped up on that spinach (Holy Spirit) the devil takes off running because he knows he's already defeated.

It is the indwelling of the Holy Spirit which gives believers the power to overcome the world. Like Popeye, we can't do it on our own. We need the Holy Spirit to help us do the will of God. Take a look:

Colossians 3:5
"Put to death, therefore, whatever belongs to your earthly nature: sexual immorality, impurity, lust, evil desires and greed, which is idolatry.

Here, the Apostle Paul tells us that the earthly nature and the deeds that it typically produces are too strong for our mere human will power to resist. But Christ living within us can overcome the earthly nature. By increasing our trust in Christ, his Spirit increasingly gives us the strength to follow his commands.

As we develop our relationship with Christ Jesus, the earthly nature is overshadowed and the new creation comes in to dominate. As you can tell from reading the prior chapters, there are many out-of-control leaders and believers in the Body of Christ. This does not mean they have not been called into the service of the Lord, but they definitely need to be delivered from their worldly ways.

The Lord said the gifts are disbursed to each one at the time we are born, and will never be taken back, but they can be quenched, like putting out a pilot light on a stove. The pilot light is still there but it has to be re-lit.

Romans 8:2-14 states that Spirit-filled believers can still sin but do not do so under the control of the Holy Spirit. Just because we are filled with the Spirit does not mean we will automatically surrender to his control. As believers we must obey God and ask his help to do so.

According to the Apostle Paul, we can be in the Spirit, but not live according to the Spirit. For example you can live in Mexico but not live according to Mexico's ways.

Ephesians 5:18 also declares that Christians are new creatures in Christ, but they are also still flesh and blood humans, vulnerable to the weakness and temptations that affect all flesh. Living in the flesh is influenced by the habits and thinking patterns that we acquired before coming into Christ. It is possible that some of the leaders with predatory behaviors were never called, or they were called but not ready to be sent out. They might have advanced on their own without God's approval, which can have the same disastrous effects as having never been called at all.

When leaders move forward before God's approval and were never truly delivered of their old-flesh patterns, they can very easily fall into the hands of the enemy and cause a lot of harm to the church and shame to Christ. People flee from such churches and never return.

Now, when the Lord began to pull me out of the world, he said, "I do answer prayers, but I never taught you how to dance because I wanted to teach you how to dance for me, not the world." Praise dance is a form of worship. Christ wanted me to worship him, not the idols and images of world. Today, I'm so over Prince and so over the world. When I finally began to dance openly and fluidly, it was nothing but the move of God.

Chapter 14

Medicine

For Modern Man

Back in October, 2011, I was in the middle of an interview to promote my first book, **Predator**, when the interviewer asked what inspired me to write the book. At that moment, the Holy Spirit spoke to me and said, "Predators need to receive me."

The Holy Spirit continued speaking to me during those moments, and he said, "Their behavior is nothing but a cry for help. I see their tears. They are only acting out because deep down inside, they need help just as much as their victims do."

Somewhere along their path in life, they experienced something traumatic which caused their predatory behavior. For example: rejection, sexual abuse, verbal abuse, physical abuse and childhood neglect.

Some may have suffered from a lack of love, which can be just as devastating as starving someone to death, and worse, if you are a child. Just ask any FBI agent in the Profiler Unit. Serial killers were 'groomed' in the home at a very young age because they were thrown away by something or someone. In fact, the FBI is packed full with files proving the direct link between childhood abuse and the killer's need to kill, in order to relieve his own pain. Church predators are the milder version of the serial killer because they kill souls.

As a hair stylist in Los Angeles, I found over the years that most of my clients suffer daily of anger, depression, hatred and mistrust, all of which cause low self-esteem, chaos, destruction and misery in their personal lives. The list goes on and on.

They experienced a great deal of pain, either in their childhood, in later relationships, or both. Others had parents or guardians that never prepared them properly for the real world. In other words, they were spoiled. For example, I meet women all the time who spoil their sons. When they became adults, it was difficult to get these young men to move out. Now they don't want to work and support themselves. When Mom finally says "Enough is enough," they go out and find women to prey on. Now, their new women pay for rent, food, utilities and clothing. Some women even fight each other to keep men like this around because they suddenly feel needed.

Invariably, these young men prey on women who suffer of low self-esteem, move into their homes, and use them to replace their mothers. The women in question soon find themselves doing everything their mothers used to do, short of changing their diapers.

This repeat cycle of behaviors is just like any other sickness or disease but the men in question can be treated for their condition. I want you to keep one thing in mind: predators can be forgiven for their behaviors. We serve a God who is full of grace and mercy and he is a forgiving God. Predators have only to acknowledge the fact that their behavior is ungodly and unpleasing to

Lakevia Amey

God, repent and turn away from their ways and they will be forgiven. Believers must continue to pray for our fellow sisters, brothers and leaders in Christ so that they will not fall into the hands of the enemy.

Victims of predators also need to receive healing. Both predators and victims have cried so much behind closed doors, they have no tears left. The Lord said our tears are all prayers to him, and each time the predator and victim cry, they are telling the Lord, "My heart is in so much pain."

Having myself experienced an impossible amount of pain in my lifetime, I started to become immune to the pain. To understand what I mean, perhaps you would care to read my first book, *Predator*.

For a long time, the pain never went away; because I hardly ever took my medication (the word of God).

At times, the pain came back stronger and stronger. Now I realize it never left me. It was just lying there in my heart, dormant for seasons at a time. I could never seem to escape and it continued to haunt me for years. This is how the enemy keeps us in bondage. Before long, I cried out, "Please Lord, I need morphine!"

I tried to stop the pain on my own but that didn't work. I finally realized that the living word is the only way to stop all pain completely. I realized that I had to give up the burden of the pain and let go of it. It was like making a 'decision' to give it up. Besides, the burden is not ours to bare; it's the Lord's.

When we try to handle our own traumas instead of turning them over to the Lord, it's like carrying a back-pack full of bricks, which soon becomes the brick-sack affecting every aspect of our lives.

As predators and victims begin to feast on the word of God and apply it to their lives, they will gain immense power. It's possible for them to live clear and pain-free of the constant pain that pulls them down. The secret to being released is staying in the word. Take a look:

Joshua 1:8
This Book of the Law shall not depart from your mouth, but you shall meditate in it day and night, that you may observe to do according to all that is written in it. For then you will make your way prosperous, and then you will have good success.

Staying in the word and in the presence of the Lord causes us to be at peace and prosper. Our thinking and speaking also becomes more powerful. For example, instead of reflecting constantly on my pain, I made a conscious decision to reflect only on my healing. Take a look:

> I hear you as I read your word, Lord. It speaks to my heart and comforts me. I can rely on your word when I'm hurting. It's like a prescription for medication prescribed by a doctor. Your word relieves my symptoms and my pain.

Today, I continue to stand on the word of God and speak healing over my life. What I'm doing is speaking my healing into existence, in the same way that God spoke in the Book of Genesis. By his spoken word, all creation came into existence. We have that same power, and can actually speak healing into our beings. The Apostle Paul confirms the power of the spoken word this way:

Romans 4:17

As it is written, "I have made you a father of many nations," in the presence of God, who gives life to the dead, and calls those things which do not exist, as though they did.

In the above verse, Paul endorsed the power of the spoken word. To illustrate this supernatural power more fully, let's revisit the astounding event concerning Jesus and the Roman Centurion in Matthew Chapter 8. One day, Jesus and the disciples entered Capernaum, the city of heathen temples and bustling commerce.

Suddenly, a man came running towards them, shouting and waving his arms in the distance. When the man finally caught up with Jesus, he said:

"Rabbi, come quick! My master is sending for you. His best servant is violently sick and needs your healing touch!"

The master this person was referring to was a Roman Centurion, a heathen, a ruler of the world, the symbol of corruption and power-lust. Now, Jesus tried to go with the man right away but he said:

"No, please sir, don't go into the house. The master said his house is not worthy for you to enter. Please just send only your word, and we know that his servant will be healed."

The out-of-breath man continued, "My master said that, like you, he understands authority. He tells this one 'do this' and he does it, and to another 'go do that' and he does it. Therefore, speak only the word and my master knows his servant will be healed!"

Now listen to Jesus' reaction. "Disciples, did you hear that? I tell you this; I have never seen such faith anywhere, not even in all of Israel!"

Although the Centurion was an unholy marauder, he displayed a militant, "weapons-grade" faith that actually shocked Jesus!

"Speak the word only and I know my servant will be healed!"

Jesus turned to the sweaty man and said, "Go and tell your master that his servant is healed."

As the man turned and ran back up the hill, the disciples heard great shouting coming from the Centurion's house. No doubt, the beloved servant was healed at that very moment. The unholy Roman Centurion knew that by his own spoken word he gave permission to Jesus of Nazareth to heal the servant.

For this reason, your spoken word is so very crucial when it comes to your own healing. Instead of speaking words of pain over yourself, begin to speak words of healing. Give the Lord permission to wash you clean of the pain.

I spoke healing over my soul and soon found myself coming back to life. Today, I am alive and well. I've been healed of pain. A miracle has been performed in my heart and emotions. I take my medication daily (the word of God) as prescribed by the Great Physician, and today I am pain free. The word of God does change lives but believers must be doers of the word also not just hearers of the word. Many times we have to participate in our own healing!

Imagine yourself carrying a fifty pound box of bricks and someone comes along to carry them for you. You are practically collapsing under the weight of the box but you say, "No, no, I need to carry these bricks! Don't help me!"

Lakevia Amey

As we read the word and get a better understanding, we must apply it to our lives. It's also important for believers to make feasting on the word part of their lifestyle, because the word is what keeps us standing strong.

There are four Gospels in the New Testament: Matthew, Mark, Luke and John. These four Gospels list 35 miracles that Christ performed. Throughout the ministry of Christ, he healed people more than anything else. In fact, Christ had a healing and deliverance ministry and still does today. This means, the Lord's intention is to heal us still today, and we have the same right to those New Testament miracles!

We know this will never change because Hebrew 13:8 declares, "Jesus Christ is the same yesterday and today." He is immutable and will never change.

Matthew 4:23-25

Jesus went throughout Galilee, teaching in their synagogues, preaching the good news of the kingdom, and healing every disease and sickness among the people. News about him spread all over Syria and people brought to him all who were ill with various disease; those suffering severe pain, the demon-possessed, those with seizures, and the paralyzed, and he healed them all. Large crowds from Galilee, the Decapolis, Jerusalem, Judea and the region across the Jordan followed him.

Today, people are still being healed by the Lord physically, emotionally, mentally, and financially. The reason is, he needs us to be fit, strong, healthy and prosperous in every area of our lives so that we can properly advertise his name in all the Earth. In fact, the health and success that he provides for us, sets us apart from any other people on Earth. Therefore, it's very important for us to become healthy in every area of our lives.

Jesus said in John 14:12, "I tell you the truth, anyone who has faith in me will do what I have been doing. In fact, he will do even greater things than these!"

This very statement is perhaps the most astounding thing ever written in the history of humankind. Here the

Lord admits that we have the exact powers that he does, if only we will practice and develop them. After all, what else could he have meant, when he said, "and greater things than these shall you do."

The miracles performed by believers can be the same as those performed by the Lord according to his own admission, only our scope will be greater when multiplied through the growth of the church. The Book of Acts describes the early beginnings of the Lord's prediction.

If Christ abides in you today, and you abide in him, you don't have to get into a prayer line to receive a healing. You have the authority to lay hands on yourself and ask for it. Remember, it is not you doing the work. It is the Holy Spirit working through you. Man is only a vessel being used, because Christ isn't physically here.

In the Book of Acts, the Apostles healed multitudes of people. Acts 5:15 describes people bringing the sick into the streets and laying them on cots and mats, in case Peter's shadow might fall on them as he passed by. Peter was known as a man of God empowered to heal. For this reason people tried to get as close to him as possible. They were drawn to his anointing.

Benny Hinn is a perfect example of a modern day Peter. When people respond by faith, God responds back to them through various ways to meet their needs.

In Acts 13:3

After they fasted and prayed, they placed
their hands on them and sent him off.

The laying on of hands is a basic, Christian practice, suggesting that it is more than mere symbolism. Jesus and his disciples didn't do it for show; they did it for the sake of results. Touching connects people to God's power. The power of the Holy Spirit flowed from the Lord's touch. The act of laying on hands is an ordained means of receiving the healing.

Luke 6:19

And the people all tried to touch him because
power flowed from him and healed them all.

Chapter 15

Hearts In So Much Pain

Readers, I don't know about you, but it seems to me that all the characters in this book were in dire need of intervention and healing. Scripture tells us to become wise, and along with wisdom, practice mercy.

Proverbs 4:7
Wisdom is the principal thing; therefore, get wisdom, and in all your getting, get understanding.

Most Christians believe the word 'understanding' means to 'get smart.' However, in the original Hebrew text this means 'consideration,' or more specifically:

'mercy; to have the deep consideration of another person's heart-breaking predicament. Let's flip the coin and consider just for one moment the predator's path in life.

The Green Card Predator in Chapter 2 was tormented with the fear of having to go back to Africa. Many regions of Africa are fraught with witchcraft, gross poverty and hopelessness. Who knows what he would be sent back to?

The minister in Chapter 3 battled a drug addiction and the pain in his soul was obviously stronger than the welfare of his own children. The homeless woman living at the motel had been abused early in life and became destitute as a result of two, bad marriages. And now, begging had become her normal way of life.

The carnal-minded pastor of Chapter 4 who chased after Sparkle never forgave his father for leaving his mother, and became a womanizer, just like his father. Notice also that Sparkle, a self-professed heathen, displayed more intelligence and crisp logic than countless, seasoned Christians in the church!

The She-Predator of Chapter 8, although beautiful, was a single mother struggling to make ends meet, and was searching for someone to help her financially. Women in her line of work always are. The man she became involved with at the church had no self-esteem, nor was he ever taught his own worth in the Lord.

And then we come to the Sofa Bandit of Chapter 10. He camped out sofas all over town, was unemployed and blind in one eye. When his father abandoned his mother, she became physically and verbally abusive toward him, as did every other woman he ever got involved with. In fact, he believes the blindness in his one eye was due to the abuse at the hand of his mother. He was a weary sole looking for a place to rest his head; preferably on a soft, cushy sofa.

Next, we come to the young man in Chapter 11 who met the Jezebel at a nightclub and became trapped by her unholy devices. He grew up in a family of hypocritical Christians that he could never trust, and yet, he married the very thing that he feared most; another deceiver.

Then, we've got Ms. Stephanie Smith in Chapter 12; the young lady that was sexually abused by her stepfather, got pregnant at a very early age, and ended up with men just like her father, time after time. The weariness and repeat assaults against her soul caused her to make a near-fatal decision, the same assaults that have caused millions to fall into sin.

Notice any patterns here? We need to obtain wisdom and mercy to understand these people. Dysfunction has its roots in abuse, and hospitals (churches) seem to be filled with these hurting people (patients). The good news is, if they could just find a clean, solid church to attend, one where the leadership and its elders place the Lord first, they would be in the right place to get well, if they truly wanted to receive healing.

But, not all patients want to receive their healing. Some go to the hospital (church) knowing they are sick, refuse treatment and check themselves out. Once a patient has been diagnosed, the doctor prescribes their medication, discusses treatment options, or informs the patient that they need to prolong their stay in the hospital.

If the patient refuses treatment for whatever reason, he must sign a discharge document. Therefore, if the patient leaves the hospital, gets sick and dies (spiritually, or otherwise) it's not the doctor's fault. The patient chose to leave; the doctor did not make that choice for him.

Likewise, God does not force himself on anyone. We have the free will to choose. We can do things his way and live pain-free, or do it our way, which will only result in heartbreak.

We have now been armed with weapons-grade information. So which shall it be? Shall we step down from the treadmill of ignorance? Shall we continue to be victimized until there is no flesh left on our bones? Or, shall we keep our eyes wide open and step into the center of God's will? Maybe it's time to shout...

"Stop! Or I'll shoot!"

We hope that you enjoyed this
frank and informative discussion with
Evangelist Lakevia Amey.

If you would like to correspond with
Evangelist Amey, buy additional copies,
book speaking engagements or
check for book-signing dates, go to:

www.lakevia.com

Visit Lakevia on Facebook

Search for: Church Predator

On You Tube, go to:

Lakevia Predator

Lakevia's books are also available on:

Amazon/books

The Prayer of Restoration

Dear God in Heaven:

I come to You in the name of Your son, Jesus
I am sorry for my sins and the life that I've been living
Please forgive me for all my sins
I believe that Jesus Christ is Your Only Son
That He shed His blood on the cross
And that He died for my sins
I need help turning from my sins
Please give me the power to do so
You said in Your scripture, Romans 10:9, that if
I confess the Lord Jesus as the Son of God, and believe
In my heart that You raised Him from the dead, I will be saved
You also promised to fill me with Your Holy Spirit
Therefore, fill me now, Lord, and give me all the
Spiritual gifts You have reserved just for me
Right now, I confess Jesus as the Lord of my soul
I believe He was raised from the dead
I also believe that according to Your promise
I am now saved and that I have eternal life
Thank You Jesus for your unlimited grace toward me
Thank you also because you will transform my life
Help me to bring glory and honor to Your name.
Amen.

www.ingramcontent.com/pod-product-compliance
Lightning Source LLC
Chambersburg PA
CBHW051831090426
42736CB00011B/1755